Homemade Pickles & Relishes

By Betsy McCracken
with the Food Editors of Farm Journal

COUNTRYSIDE PRESS
a division of Farm Journal, Inc.
Philadelphia, Pennsylvania

Distributed to the trade by
Two Continents Publishing Group
New York, New York

ACKNOWLEDGMENTS

The authors wish to express appreciation to Gerald D. Kuhn, Ph.D. and Louise W. Hamilton, R.D. of the Pennsylvania State University Extension staff for reviewing *How to Make Successful Pickles*—also for their scientific expertise in the most up-to-date techniques and processing procedures for homemade pickles and relishes.

Book Design: Karen Ketchel
Cover Design: Alfred Casciato
Cover Photo: William Hazzard/Hazzard Studio

Copyright 1976 by Farm Journal, Inc.
All rights reserved
Printed in the United States of America

Library of Congress Catalog Card Number 76-14048

Contents

CHAPTER I: How to Make Successful Pickles — 5

CHAPTER II: Perfect Cucumber Pickles — 19

CHAPTER III: Tangy Vegetables — 45

CHAPTER IV: Spicy Fruits — 62

CHAPTER V: Piquant Relishes — 79

CHAPTER VI: Peppy Sauces — 101

CHAPTER VII: Easy Freezer & Refrigerator Specialties — 114

INDEX — 125

CHAPTER I

How to Make Successful Pickles

Your summertime garden or nearby roadside stand can be the source of a most inexpensive way to add flavor, color, and an extra-special touch to year-round family and company meals. There's almost no limit to the fruits and vegetables you can turn into a variety of outstanding pickles and relishes.

Country women have long been famous for their heirloom pickles, such as Piccalilli, Bread-and-Butter Pickles, and crisp dill pickles. Recipes were somewhat sketchy—even the same recipe would give a variation in success (or failure). Extensive research has taken the guesswork out of pickling vegetables and fruits. Discoveries, applied to tests in home kitchens as well as in laboratories, have practically eliminated the chance of failure. Now, even the novice at pickling can successfully make the tested recipes in this book.

But there are definite rules for success. You have to use fresh, high-quality ingredients. You must process pickles in a boiling water canner for the precise time specified in updated recipes. You must use recommended equipment—you cannot depend on the old-fashioned open-kettle way of canning because there is danger of spoilage from organisms that enter the food when you transfer it from kettle to jar. All homemade pickle products must be processed in a boiling water canner to destroy these organisms as well as enzymes in fruits and vegetables that affect the keeping quality and flavor when pickled. And the heat of the boiling water canner helps insure a good seal between lid and canning jars.

Modern Pickle Recipes

For successful and safe pickling, use modern methods and modern recipes and follow all instructions carefully. When we say modern recipes, we mean recipes that have been tested for their acid level to be sure that they have a final pH of 4.2 or less.

If you follow the directions in this chapter for all steps in making pickles and pickle products, you will end up with excellent flavor and keeping quality.

The Five Types of Pickles

• **Brined or fermented pickles** go through a curing process that can last from 3 to 5 weeks. The white interior of cucumbers becomes translucent, the outside an olive green. Flavor may be enhanced by adding dill, garlic or spices.

The strength of the brine is very important. You should maintain a 10 percent brine solution. Too strong a brine at the beginning can inhibit growth of certain bacteria that produce lactic acid, causing shriveled pickles with a poor flavor. Too weak a brine causes the desirable bacteria to be overcome by spoilage bacteria, resulting in slippery pickles with a poor flavor.

Maintaining the proper brine strength is the secret to fermenting pickles successfully. Salt draws moisture from the cucumbers, which dilutes the brine so that it becomes weak. The correct amount of salt must be added in correct amounts throughout the fermentation period.

To prevent vegetables floating to the top of the brine, hold them down under the brine with a heavy plate or glass lid. Place a glass canning jar filled with water on the plate. Be sure to apply a lid and screw band to the filled jar of water to prevent evaporation or accidental spillage of water into the brine.

The correct temperature during the fermentation process is also important. Keep temperature between 65° and 75°F to encourage development of the desirable bacteria.

Remove scum daily from brine surface. Scum interferes with the fermentation process.

- **Fresh-pack or quick-process** pickles are vegetables or fruits, either whole or cut up, brined for several hours or overnight. They are then put into vinegar solution and processed.
- **Relishes** are prepared from chopped fruits or vegetables, seasoned and cooked to the desired thickness before packing into jars and processed. Sauces are similar, but of finer consistency.
- **Fruit pickles** are usually prepared from whole fruits and simmered in spicy, sweet-sour syrup. Then they are packed and processed.
- **Freezer and refrigerator specialties** both fruit and vegetable, are real time-savers because the processing can be skipped.

Step I—Select Top-Quality Ingredients

Fruits and Vegetables
- Select young, tender, freshly gathered fruits and vegetables for pickling. A good rule to follow is to make pickles the same day as the produce is harvested. Delays in canning fresh produce reduce their quality and give the bacteria on food an opportunity to multiply, making it more difficult to process safely.

If you cannot handle your produce the same day as harvested, refrigerate it or keep it in a cool, airy place. This is particularly important with cucumbers. They deteriorate rapidly at room temperature.

Cucumbers should be of a pickling variety because not all cucumbers are suitable for pickling. Cucumbers that are used for eating plain or adding to a salad are called slicers. They are frequently larger with thick skins and tend to result in a soft pickle with a tough skin. For a crisper pickle, we do advise using pickling cucumbers in our recipes. The garden slicer variety may be used, but be sure that the cucumbers are no longer than 3 to 4 inches. Never use cucumbers that have been waxed because the brine cannot penetrate the skin.

Pickling cucumbers are thin-skinned and more uniform in size and shape. Some of the most popular pickling cucumbers are Ohio MR 17, West India Gherkins, Wisconsin SMR and the Burpee Pickler. Choose cucumbers that are slightly immature. However, fruits used in pickling should be fully ripened, but firm. Underripe fruit is not as sweet as fully ripened and much of the natural flavor has not developed.

- Discard all small fruits that show even a tiny bit of mold, such as cherries, plums and berries. All other fruits should be carefully selected and trimmed free of diseased spots before using in recipes.
- Wash all fruits and vegetables thoroughly even if they are to be pared. Dirt contains some of the most difficult bacteria to kill and encourages molds and yeasts to grow on the outer surface. Wash small lots at a time, under running water or through several changes of water. Lift the food out of the water each time so that the dirt that has been washed off won't go back onto the food. Do not let produce soak in the water; it may lose flavor and food value. Handle fruits and vegetables gently to avoid bruising.
- Remove any bruised or decayed areas on large fruits well below and around the defective areas as some of

the surrounding tissue may be soured. Small amounts of spoiled food put into a canning jar and processed can cause a complete jar of food to spoil later on.
- Trim a ⅛-inch slice from both ends of cucumbers. The ends contain enzymes that may cause pickles to soften.
- Prevent darkening of fruits and vegetables by heating the food as rapidly as possible after cutting, to destroy enzymes that cause discoloration. Some fruits and vegetables such as apples, peaches and pears darken rapidly. Submerge these fruits in a solution of 2 tablespoons vinegar and 2 tablespoons salt per gallon of water. Fruit-Fresh, a commercial antioxidant, may be used. Follow directions on the label. Work quickly. Don't soak food more than 20 minutes. Drain and rinse before heating and/or packing in jars.

Salt

Use pure granulated pickling or canning salt. Non-iodized table salt may be used, but ingredients added to table salt to prevent caking may make the pickle brine cloudy. Do not use iodized salt as the pickles will darken and, in brine pickles, fermentation may be retarded.

Vinegar

Use a high-grade vinegar with an acidity of 5 percent (see label for acidity percentage). Never use homemade vinegar. All the recipes in this book specify 5% acid strength vinegar. Do not reduce the amount of vinegar specified in recipes or change the proportion of vinegar to product. In other words, it is important to follow the directions exactly. If a less sour pickle is desired, add sugar rather than decrease the vinegar. It is very important that each pickle recipe have the right ratio of food to acid to obtain a safe pH. By using a weaker strength vinegar than 5 percent, the acid balance would be incorrect. It contains too little acetic acid to be used safely in recipes for pickled products. Recipes worked out for an acid level or pH reading of 4.2 will give a safe product that will keep if properly processed and sealed. *Clostridium botulinum*, which causes botulism poisoning, will *not* grow in foods with a pH of 4.5 or lower but *will* grow in foods with a higher pH.

Cider vinegar has a mellow flavor that blends well with pickling herbs and spices, but it can darken light-colored fruits and vegetables. Use white vinegar when a light color is important—with pickled pears or onions, for instance.

Sugar

White sugar is preferred for light-colored fruits and vegetables. Brown sugar may add flavor to darker pickles, however.

Spices

Be sure to used the freshest spices and herbs for superior flavor. Spices and herbs deteriorate quickly and lose their pungency in heat and humidity. Store them in an airtight container in a cool place.

Soft Water

Use soft water for making a pickling brine because the minerals in hard water will interfere with the curing process. If your water supply is hard, boil the water for 15 minutes to remove the minerals. Let it stand 24 hours. Remove scum from the top, being careful not to disturb the mineral sediment in the bottom of the container. If necessary, strain through several thicknesses of clean cheesecloth. Add 1 tablespoon of vinegar to each gallon water.

Step II—Use The Right Equipment

Canner

A boiling water canner is essential for processing pickles and all pickled products. You may use any large metal container that is deep enough to allow 1 or 2 inches of water above the jars plus extra space for boiling room. It must have a tight-fitting cover and must be equipped with a wire rack.

Glass Jars and Lids

Always use standard canning jars and lids. Check each jar carefully to be sure that it is free from cracks, chips, sharp edges or uneven sealing surface. Check canning lids for scratches, dents and rust. Defective jars and lids may prevent an airtight seal and cause spoilage. Use of jars and lids that have been used for commercially canned foods is not recommended.

Small Utensils

Here is a list of utensils that make the job of pickling easier, safer and more efficient for you.

Teakettle	Stiff brushes
Long-handled spoons	Colander or wire basket
Slotted spoon	Sieve or wire strainer
Long-handled fork	Mixing bowls
Long-handled ladle with lip	Kitchen scissors
Wide-mouthed funnel	Set of measuring spoons
Sharp butcher knife	Set of measuring cups
Sharp kitchen knife	Household scales
Vegetable peeler	Timer
Wooden cutting board	Cheesecloth
Food grinder	Jar-lifter or tongs
Small food mill	Cooling rack
Grater	

Containers

Stoneware, stainless steel, glass, pottery (but some foreign-made crocks have glazes high in lead—do not use) or unchipped enamel containers should be used for foods that remain in a vinegar or brine solution for any length of time. Do not use wooden or other metal containers or any container that is chipped or cracked.

Step III—Use Proper Canning Procedures

Preparing Jars and Lids

Pickles from recipes that call for processing times of *less than 15 minutes* in a boiling water canner must be put into sterilized jars. To sterilize jars, place them right side up on a rack in boiling water canner. Fill canner and jars with water to a level of at least 1 inch above the tops of the jars. Boil 15 minutes, starting to count the time when water reaches an active rolling boil. If possible, remove one jar at a time, empty out the water, fill with food and adjust the lid. If this is not possible, remove jars from boiling water after sterilizing and place upside down on a clean towel. This prevents microorganisms present in the air from collecting in the jars. Do not use a dishwasher to sterilize; the water is not hot enough.

It is not necessary to sterilize empty jars which will be processed in a boiling water canner for *15 minutes or longer*. The jars will be sterilized along with the food. However, even if the jars *look* clean, they should be washed in hot sudsy water (by hand or in the dishwasher) and rinsed thoroughly in hot water. Fill jars immediately or allow them to drain upside down on a clean towel. Be sure that there is no detergent powder clinging to the inside surface of the jars. Alkaline detergents may cause color changes in some foods.

Follow manufacturer's directions for preparing lids.

Filling Jars

Pack the hot jars uniformly with the pickles, making sure that the pickling liquid covers them. Food that is not covered with pickling liquid tends to darken. Hot food should be packed at or near boiling temperature and covered with boiling liquid. All raw food is also covered with *boiling* liquid. If you use a jar funnel it will help to reduce spilling. Try to keep liquid off the sealing edge of the jar. Fill each jar to the head space indicated in the recipe.

Head Space

Pickles, relishes, sauces and purees need ¼-inch head space. This means that you fill the jar up to ¼-inch of the top—no more, no less. Too little head space may force liquid out of the jars during the processing. This may cause food particles to adhere to the sealing edge, which will result in an imperfect seal. Too much head space allows too much air inside the jar. This can cause gases to form and food may discolor.

Air Bubbles

Air bubbles often become trapped inside the jars as they are being filled. You'll have a better product if you remove all air bubbles. To release bubbles, gently move a plastic spatula or knife up and down between food and jar, all the way around. Avoid using a metal knife—if it should hit the bottom of the jar it could weaken the glass and cause breakage during heat sterilization. Readjust head space after releasing bubbles.

Closing Jars

Wipe the sealing edge of the jars with a clean, damp paper towel to remove food or liquid. Any food particles left on the sealing surface could prevent the lid from sealing.

Follow the manufacturer's directions for adjusting lids. The recommended two-piece self-sealing lids must be tightened before sterilization. Tighten them firmly so that the jar lid is held closely to the sealing edge. If you notice a great many air bubbles inside jars and/or food discoloration near the top of the jar after they have been stored, it could be a sign that you might have tightened screw bands too much—you know your own grip strength, so adjust it accordingly.

Heat Sterilization—Boiling Water Canner

All pickled products must be heat sterilized in a boiling water canner in order to destroy organisms that cause spoilage and to inactivate enzymes that may affect flavor, color and texture of the final products.

To use the boiling water canner, place jars of food on a rack in canner about half-full of hot water. Add hot (not boiling) water to raise the level at least 1-inch above the jars. Put cover on canner and quickly bring water to a rolling boil.

Start to count processing time when water returns to boiling and continue to boil gently and steadily for the time recommended for the particular food being canned. Remove jars and retighten one-piece lids or screw bands if recommended by lid manufacturer.

Processing procedures for fermented cucumbers and fresh-pack dills are slightly different from the usual water canner procedures. For these products, place jars of foods on a rack in canner half-full of boiling water. Add boiling water to raise the level at least 1-inch above the jars. Start to count the processing time as soon as the filled jars are placed in the actively boiling water. This prevents development of a cooked flavor and loss of crispness.

In both procedures, always keep jars covered with at least 1-inch of boiling water. It may be necessary to add additional boiling water.

Processing times as given in the recipes in this book are for altitudes less than 1,000 feet above sea level. At altitudes of 1,000 feet or above, you need to increase recommended processing times as follows:

ALTITUDE CHART

Boiling Water Canner	Increase processing time if the time called for is:	
Altitude	20 Minutes or Less	More than 20 Minutes
1,000 feet	1 minute	2 minutes
2,000 feet	2 minutes	4 minutes
3,000 feet	3 minutes	6 minutes
4,000 feet	4 minutes	8 minutes
5,000 feet	5 minutes	10 minutes
6,000 feet	6 minutes	12 minutes
7,000 feet	7 minutes	14 minutes
8,000 feet	8 minutes	16 minutes
9,000 feet	9 minutes	18 minutes
10,000 feet	10 minutes	20 minutes

Cooling Jars

Remove jars from canner and place them upright on a rack, leaving several inches between jars to allow free air circulation. Keep out of drafts. Do not cover. Cool for 12 to 24 hours.

Check for Airtight Seal

Remove metal screw bands carefully, if you have used the 2-piece lid. If the center of the 2-piece lid has a slight dip or stays down when pressed, the jars are sealed. Tap the center of the lid with a spoon. A clear ringing sound means a good seal.

Storage of Pickle Products

Wipe jars with a clean, damp cloth and label with

product name and date. Store in a clean, cool, dark, dry area where there is no danger of freezing. Exposure to light can cause bleaching, deterioration of flavor or darkening of the product.

Check for Spoilage

You should check for signs of spoilage periodically. Examine jars closely before opening. A bulging lid or leakage may mean contents are spoiled. During and after opening a jar, look for other signs of spoilage such as spurting liquid, mold, color change, unpleasant odor, softness, mushiness or slipperiness of pickles. IF THERE IS EVEN THE SLIGHTEST INDICATION OF SPOILAGE–DO NOT EAT OR TASTE THE PRODUCT. Dispose of the contents immediately. Wash the jar in hot soapy water, rinse and then *boil the jar itself in clean water for 15 minutes* to kill spoilage bacteria for future use of jar.

Common Pickling Problems

If you follow directions carefully and use good quality fruits and vegetables, your homemade pickles and relishes should turn out successfully. Some of the common problems encountered in pickle making and their causes are:

Softening of Pickles. This is usually due to spoilage caused by bacterial action. Softening may result when:
- The brine used is too weak.
- The strength of the brine is not maintained.
- Pickles are not kept under the brine.
- Vinegar is weakened too much.
- The scum is not kept off the brine.
- Pickles are boiled.

Shriveling of Pickles. This often results when:
- The vinegar, sugar or salt solution is too strong at

the beginning (use a weaker solution at first and gradually increase the strength).
- Fruit is cooked too quickly in a strong sugar or vinegar solution, and not allowed to plump up.

Hollow Pickles. This may result from:
- Using imperfect or old cucumbers.
- Letting cucumbers stand too long between gathering and brining.

Dark Color in Pickles. This could be the result of:
- Using powdered spices.
- Using too much spice.
- Packing whole spices with pickles.
- Using iron utensils or water containing iron.
- Using iodized salt.

CHAPTER II

Perfect Cucumber Pickles

By the end of the harvest, every well-appointed preserve shelf in Grandmother's day was loaded with jars of tangy pickles and relishes. But her greatest variety of pickles were made from cucumbers, brined or sweetened, flavored with dill or spices. Today's homemakers agree that cucumbers are still the mainstay of the pickle maker.

If you grow pickling cucumbers in your garden, you already have a head start to perfect pickles. You can harvest the vegetable when it reaches the ideal size for the pickles you intend to make. And you can hurry them from vine to canning jar to retain a maximum of garden-fresh taste.

In addition to the old-time favorites, we have included some cucumber recipes for conversation-type pickles—sure to bring compliments. The Curry Pickles are a combination of thinly sliced cucumbers, onions and bright red peppers. These pickles are attractive as well as delicious and are a thoughtful homemade gift at holiday time. Spiced Sour Pickle Sticks will make a big hit when served with bubbling baked beans on a cold winter night. You'll have a feeling of pride when you serve any one of these homemade pickles—even *better* than Grandma used to make.

FRESH-PACK DILLS

9 lbs. (3 to 5-inch) pickling cucumbers
1½ c. pickling salt
2 gals. water
¾ c. pickling salt
¼ c. sugar
9 c. water
6 c. 5% acid strength vinegar
2 tblsp. pickling spices
24 heads fresh dill
Mustard seeds

Wash cucumbers; cut ⅛-inch slice off each end. (Enzymes found in ends may cause softening of pickles.) Place in large bowl. Cover with brine made by adding 1½ c. salt to 2 gals. water. Let stand overnight. Drain.

Combine ¾ c. salt, sugar, 9 c. water and vinegar in large kettle. Tie pickling spices in cheesecloth bag; add to kettle. Bring mixture to boiling.

Pack cucumbers into 8 hot quart jars. Place 3 dill heads and 2 tsp. mustard seeds in each jar. Remove spice bag from boiling liquid. Immediately pour liquid over cucumbers, filling to within ¼-inch from the top. Adjust lids.

Process in boiling water bath 15 minutes. Start to count processing time as soon as jars are placed into actively boiling water.

Remove jars. Cool on wire racks 12 to 24 hours. Check jars for airtight seal (see Chapter 1). Makes 8 quarts.

SPICED SOUR PICKLE STICKS

> 3 lbs. (4-inch) pickling cucumbers
> 6 c. 5% acid strength cider vinegar
> ½ c. sugar
> 2 tsp. pickling salt
> 2 tsp. mustard seeds
> 2 tsp. celery seeds
> ½ tsp. whole cloves
> ½ tsp. peppercorns

Wash cucumbers; cut ⅛-inch slice off each end. Slice cucumbers lengthwise into fourths. Place in crock or bowl.

Combine vinegar, sugar and salt in large saucepan. Tie mustard and celery seeds, cloves and peppercorns in cheesecloth bag. Add to kettle. Bring mixture to boiling; boil 5 minutes. Pour over cucumbers. Cover and let stand 24 hours. Remove spice bag.

Drain cucumbers, reserving liquid. Heat reserved liquid in large saucepan.

Pack cucumbers into 4 hot, sterilized pint jars. Pour boiling liquid over cucumbers, filling to within ¼-inch from the top. Adjust lids.

Process in boiling water bath 10 minutes. Start to count the processing time when water in canner returns to boiling.

Remove jars. Cool on wire racks 12 to 24 hours. Check jars for airtight seal (see Chapter 1). Makes 4 pints.

EASY KOSHER DILL PICKLES

5 lbs. (4-inch) pickling cucumbers
¾ c. pickling salt
9 c. water
3 c. 5% acid strength cider vinegar
½ tsp. mustard seeds
10 heads fresh dill
5 cloves garlic
1 large hot red pepper, cut in 5 strips

Wash cucumbers; cut ⅛-inch slice off each end.

Combine salt, water, vinegar and mustard seeds in large saucepan. Bring mixture to boiling.

Pack cucumbers in 5 hot quart jars. Place 2 heads dill, 1 clove garlic and 1 strip pepper in each jar. Pour boiling liquid over cucumbers, filling to within ¼-inch from the top. Adjust lids.

Process in boiling water bath 15 minutes. Start to count processing time as soon as jars are placed into actively boiling water.

Remove jars. Cool on wire racks 12 to 24 hours. Check jars for airtight seal (see Chapter 1). Makes 5 quarts.

CRISP-AS-ICE CUCUMBER SLICES

4 lbs. pickling cucumbers
8 onions, thinly sliced
2 green peppers, seeded and cut in strips
½ c. pickling salt
Ice cubes
4 c. sugar
4½ c. 5% acid strength vinegar
1½ tsp. ground turmeric
½ tsp. ground cloves
3½ tsp. mustard seeds

Wash cucumbers; cut ⅛-inch slice off each end. Thinly slice cucumbers, making about 4 qts. Layer cucumbers, onion, green pepper and salt in large bowl. Cover with ice cubes. Let stand 3 hours, adding more ice if needed. Drain well.

Combine sugar, vinegar, turmeric, cloves and mustard seeds in large kettle; bring to boiling. Add vegetables. Heat over low heat to scalding (do not boil). Stir mixture often to prevent scorching. Immediately ladle into 6 hot, sterilized pint jars, filling to within ¼-inch from the top. Adjust lids.

Process in boiling water bath 5 minutes. Start to count the processing time when water in canner returns to boiling.

Remove jars. Cool on wire racks 12 to 24 hours. Check jars for airtight seal (see Chapter 1). Makes 5½ pints.

SWEET PICKLE SLICES

4 lbs. pickling cucumbers
4 c. 5% acid strength vinegar
¼ c. sugar
3 tblsp. pickling salt
1 tblsp. mustard seeds
2 c. 5% acid strength vinegar
3 c. sugar
2¼ tsp. celery seeds
1 tblsp. whole allspice

Wash cucumbers; cut ⅛-inch slice off each end. Cut in ⅛-inch thick slices, making about 4 qts. Combine cucumber slices, 4 c. vinegar, ¼ c. sugar, salt and mustard seeds in large kettle. Bring mixture to boiling; reduce heat. Simmer 15 minutes or until cucumbers turn slightly yellow. Do not overcook. Drain well.

Combine 2 c. vinegar, 3 c. sugar, celery seeds and allspice in large saucepan. Bring mixture to boiling.

Pack cucumber slices into 5 hot, sterilized pint jars. Pour boiling liquid over cucumbers, filling to within ¼-inch from the top. Adjust lids.

Process in boiling water bath 5 minutes. Start to count the processing time when water in canner returns to boiling.

Remove jars. Cool on wire racks 12 to 24 hours. Check jars for airtight seal (see Chapter 1). Makes 5 pints.

PRIZE SWEET PICKLES

3½ lbs. (2½-inch) pickling cucumbers
½ c. pickling salt
1 qt. boiling water
1½ qts. 5% acid strength vinegar
2 c. water
3 c. sugar
1 tblsp. pickling spices
1 tsp. celery seeds

8 jars

Wash cucumbers; cut ⅛-inch slice off each end. Place cucumbers in large bowl. Dissolve salt in 1 qt. boiling water; pour over cucumbers. Let stand until cool. Drain well. Return cucumbers to bowl.

Combine vinegar, 2 c. water, sugar, pickling spices and celery seeds in large saucepan. Bring mixture to boiling. Pour over cucumbers. Let stand 24 hours.

Place cucumbers and liquid in large saucepan; bring to boiling. Immediately pack into 4 hot, sterilized pint jars, filling to within ¼-inch from the top. Adjust lids.

Process in boiling water bath 10 minutes. Start to count the processing time when water in canner returns to boiling.

Remove jars. Cool on wire racks 12 to 24 hours. Check jars for airtight seal (see Chapter 1). Makes 4 pints.

CHEERFUL SWEET PICKLES

9 yellow pickling cucumbers, pared
½ c. pickling salt
3½ qts. water
3½ c. sugar
2 c. 5% acid strength vinegar
1 tsp. whole cloves
2 sticks cinnamon
1 (4 oz.) jar maraschino cherries
2 tsp. red food color

Cut ⅛-inch slice off each end of pared cucumbers. Seed cucumbers and cut into cubes, making about 9 c. cubes. Place cucumbers in large bowl; sprinkle with salt. Cover with water. Let stand overnight.

Place cucumbers and liquid in large saucepan. Heat to boiling; drain well. Combine sugar and vinegar in large saucepan. Tie cloves and cinnamon in cheesecloth bag; add to saucepan. Heat to boiling. Pour over cucumbers in large bowl. Let stand overnight.

Place cucumbers and liquid in large kettle. Heat to boiling. Simmer until cucumbers are tender (do not overcook). Add undrained cherries and food color. Immediately ladle into 4 hot, sterilized pint jars, filling to within ¼-inch from the top. Adjust lids.

Process in boiling water bath 5 minutes. Start to count the processing time when water in canner returns to boiling.

Remove jars. Cool on wire racks 12 to 24 hours. Check jars for airtight seal (see Chapter 1). Makes 4 pints.

SWEET DILLS

4 lbs. (3 to 5-inch) pickling cucumbers
6 c. 5% acid strength vinegar
6 c. sugar
6 tblsp. pickling salt
1½ tsp. celery seeds
1½ tsp. mustard seeds
2 large onions, thinly sliced
16 heads fresh dill

Wash cucumbers; cut ⅛-inch slice off each end. Cut cucumbers in ¼-inch crosswise slices.

Combine vinegar, sugar, salt, celery and mustard seeds in large kettle. Bring mixture to boiling.

Place 2 slices onion and 1 dill head in each of 8 hot pint jars. Pack cucumber slices into jars. Place 1 slice onion and 1 head dill on top. Pour boiling liquid over cucumbers, filling to within ¼-inch from the top. Adjust lids.

Process in boiling water bath 15 minutes. Start to count processing time as soon as jars are placed into actively boiling water.

Remove jars. Cool on wire racks 12 to 24 hours. Check jars for airtight seal (see Chapter 1). Makes 8 pints.

HAMBURGER DILL CHIPS

4 lbs. (4-inch) pickling cucumbers
4½ c. water
1 qt. 5% acid strength white vinegar
6 tblsp. pickling salt
16 heads fresh dill
Mustard seeds
16 peppercorns

Wash cucumbers; cut ⅛-inch slice off each end. Cut cucumbers into ¼-inch crosswise slices.

Combine water, vinegar and salt in large saucepan; bring to boiling.

Pack cucumbers in 8 hot pint jars. Add 2 dill heads, ½ tsp. mustard seeds and 2 peppercorns to each jar. Pour boiling liquid over cucumbers, filling to within ¼-inch from the top. Adjust lids.

Process in boiling water bath 15 minutes. Start to count processing time as soon as jars are placed into actively boiling water.

Remove jars. Cool on wire racks 12 to 24 hours. Check jars for airtight seals (see Chapter 1). Makes 8 pints.

BEST-EVER BREAD-AND-BUTTERS

40 to 50 pickling cucumbers
½ c. pickling salt
Ice cubes
1 qt. 5% acid strength vinegar
4 c. sugar
2 tblsp. mustard seeds
1 tblsp. celery seeds
1 tblsp. ground ginger
1 tsp. ground turmeric
½ tsp. white pepper
2 qts. sliced onions

Wash cucumbers; cut ⅛-inch slice off each end. Slice cucumbers, making about 4 qts. Layer cucumber slices and salt in large bowl. Cover with ice cubes. Let stand 2 to 3 hours or until cucumbers are crisp and cold. Add more ice if needed. Drain well.

Combine vinegar, sugar, mustard seeds, celery seeds, ginger, turmeric and pepper in large kettle. Bring mixture to boiling; boil 10 minutes. Add cucumbers and onion; bring back to boiling. Immediately pack into 8 hot pint jars, filling to within ¼-inch from the top. Adjust lids.

Process in boiling water bath 15 minutes. Start to count the processing time when water in canner returns to boiling.

Remove jars. Cool on wire racks 12 to 24 hours. Check jars for airtight seal (see Chapter 1). Makes 8 pints.

CURRY PICKLES

6 large pickling cucumbers, pared
10 medium onions
2 large sweet red peppers
½ c. pickling salt
4 c. sugar
2 c. 5% acid strength vinegar
1 c. water
3 tblsp. pickling spices
2 tblsp. celery salt
1 tsp. curry powder

Cut ⅛-inch slice off each end of pared cucumber. Cut cucumbers, onion and peppers into thin slices; place in large bowl. Sprinkle with salt. Add enough cold water to cover. Let stand overnight. Drain well.

Combine sugar, vinegar and water in large kettle. Tie pickling spices in cheesecloth bag. Add spice bag, vegetables and celery salt to kettle. Bring mixture to boiling; boil 15 to 30 minutes. Add curry powder. Immediately ladle into 7 hot, sterilized pint jars, filling to within ¼-inch from the top. Adjust lids.

Process in boiling water bath 5 minutes. Start to count the processing time when water in canner returns to boiling.

Remove jars. Cool on wire racks 12 to 24 hours. Check jars for airtight seal (see Chapter 1). Makes 6½ pints.

PICKLES AND ONIONS

8 (4-inch) pickling cucumbers
¾ lb. small white onions or
   2½ c. sliced onion
5% acid strength vinegar
Water
2 c. sugar
2 c. 5% acid strength vinegar
5 tsp. pickling salt

Wash cucumbers; cut ⅛-inch slice off each end. Cut in 1-inch chunks. Place cucumbers and onions in large kettle. Cover with equal parts of vinegar and water; bring to boiling. Remove from heat; drain well.

Meanwhile, combine sugar and 2 c. vinegar in medium saucepan; bring to boiling.

Pack cucumbers and onions into 5 hot, sterilized half-pint jars. Add 1 tsp. salt to each jar. Pour boiling liquid over cucumbers, filling to within ¼-inch from the top. Adjust lids.

Process in boiling water bath 5 minutes. Start to count the processing time when water in canner returns to boiling.

Remove jars. Cool on wire racks 12 to 24 hours. Check for airtight seal (see Chapter 1). Makes 5 half-pints.

FRENCH SOUR PICKLES

2 lbs. (3-inch) pickling cucumbers
3 tblsp. pickling salt
2 qts. water
3 c. 5% acid strength white vinegar
4 small white onions, peeled
4 small cloves garlic
4 tsp. mustard seeds

Wash cucumbers; cut ⅛-inch slice off each end. Place cucumbers in large bowl. Sprinkle with salt and cover with water. Let stand 24 hours; drain well.

Heat vinegar in medium saucepan to boiling.

Pack cucumbers in 4 hot, sterilized pint jars. Place 1 onion, 1 clove garlic and 1 tsp. mustard seeds in each jar. Pour boiling vinegar over cucumbers, filling to within ¼-inch from the top. Adjust lids.

Process in boiling water bath 10 minutes. Start to count the processing time when water in the canner returns to boiling.

Remove jars. Cool on wire racks 12 to 24 hours. Check jars for airtight seal (see Chapter 1). Makes 4 pints.

EASY PICKLE CHUNKS

2 lbs. (4 to 5-inch) pickling cucumbers
1⅔ c. 5% acid strength white vinegar
1 c. water
1 c. sugar
2 tblsp. pickling salt
2 tblsp. mustard seeds
2 tsp. celery seeds
1 tsp. curry powder

Wash cucumbers; cut ⅛-inch slice off each end. Cut cucumbers into ¾-inch chunks.

Combine vinegar, water, sugar, salt, mustard seeds, celery seeds and curry powder in large kettle. Bring mixture to boiling. Add cucumbers; heat again just to boiling. Immediately ladle into 4 hot, sterilized pint jars, filling to within ¼-inch from the top. Adjust lids.

Process in boiling water bath 10 minutes. Start to count processing time when water in the canner returns to boiling.

Remove jars. Cool on wire racks 12 to 24 hours. Check jars for airtight seal (see Chapter 1). Makes 4 pints.

PARSLEY PICKLE CHUNKS

      4 lbs. (3 to 4-inch) pickling cucumbers
      ¼ c. pickling salt
      3 c. 5% acid strength cider vinegar
      3 c. water
      3 c. sugar
      2 tsp. mixed pickling spices
      2 tsp. celery seeds
      2 large bunches fresh parsley sprigs

Cut cucumbers in ½-inch chunks, discarding ⅛-inch slice off each end.

Combine cucumber chunks and salt in large bowl. Cover with cold water; let stand 24 hours. Drain well.

Combine vinegar, water, sugar, pickling spices and celery seeds in large saucepan. Bring to boiling.

Place a layer of parsley sprigs in bottom of each 8 hot pint jars. Pack cucumber chunks into jars, placing a layer of parsley in the middle and on top. Pour boiling liquid over cucumbers, filling to within ¼-inch from the top. Adjust lids.

Process in boiling water bath 15 minutes. Start to count processing time as soon as jars are placed into actively boiling water.

Remove jars. Cool on wire racks 12 to 24 hours. Check jars for airtight seal (see Chapter 1). Makes 8 pints.

EXTRA GOOD SWEET DILLS

4½ lbs. (4-inch) pickling cucumbers
Ice water
2 c. 5% acid strength cider vinegar
1 c. water
1 c. sugar
2 tblsp. pickling salt
¼ c. dill seeds
1 medium onion, thinly sliced

Wash cucumbers; cut ⅛-inch slice off each end. Cover with ice water and let stand 3 to 4 hours. Drain; cut in lengthwise strips.

Combine vinegar, 1 c. water, sugar and salt in medium saucepan. Bring mixture to boiling.

Pack cucumbers into 4 hot pint jars. Add 1 tblsp. dill seeds and 2 slices onion to each jar. Pour boiling liquid over cucumbers, filling to within ¼-inch from the top. Adjust lids.

Process in boiling water bath 15 minutes. Start to count processing time as soon as jars are placed into actively boiling water.

Remove jars. Cool on wire racks 12 to 24 hours. Check jars for airtight seal (see Chapter 1). Makes 4 pints.

MUSTARD SANDWICH PICKLES

4 lbs. medium pickling cucumbers
6 medium white onions, thinly sliced
1 c. pickling salt
3½ c. sugar
¾ c. flour
½ c. dry mustard
1½ tsp. ground turmeric
1 tsp. celery seeds
1 qt. 5% acid strength cider vinegar

Wash cucumbers; cut ⅛-inch slice off each end. Slice cucumbers, making about 4 qts. Layer cucumbers, onions and salt in large bowl; cover with cold water. Let stand overnight; drain. Rinse well with cold water.

Combine sugar, flour, mustard, turmeric and celery seeds in large kettle. Gradually blend in vinegar. Cook, stirring constantly, until mixture comes to a boil. Add vegetables and cook, stirring frequently, until mixture returns to boiling. Pack immediately into 8 hot, sterilized pint jars, filling to within ¼-inch from the top. Adjust lids.

Process in boiling water bath 5 minutes. Start to count the processing time when water in canner returns to boiling.

Remove jars. Cool on wire racks 12 to 24 hours. Check jars for airtight seal (see Chapter 1). Makes 8 pints.

YELLOW CUCUMBER STICKS

10 lbs. large yellow pickling cucumbers
⅓ c. pickling salt
1 qt. 5% acid strength vinegar
2 c. sugar
2 tblsp. pickling spices
2 tblsp. mustard seeds
1 tsp. celery seeds

Pare cucumbers; cut ⅛-inch slice off each end. Cut cucumbers in half lengthwise. Scrape out seeds. Cut in 1x2-inch sticks; place in large bowl. Sprinkle with salt; add enough cold water to cover. Let stand overnight. Drain; rinse well with cold water.

Combine vinegar and sugar in large kettle. Tie pickling spices, mustard and celery seeds in cheesecloth bag; add to kettle. Bring to boiling; boil 5 minutes.

Add cucumber sticks. Return to boiling; reduce heat. Simmer 25 minutes or until cucumbers are tender and translucent. Remove spice bag. Immediately ladle mixture into 6 hot, sterilized pint jars, filling to within ¼-inch from the top. Adjust lids.

Process in boiling water bath 5 minutes. Start to count the processing time when water in canner returns to boiling.

Remove jars. Cool on wire racks 12 to 24 hours. Check jars for airtight seal (see Chapter 1). Makes 6 pints.

Note: For colorful holiday pickles, tint cucumber sticks by adding ½ tsp. red or green food color to vinegar mixture.

FOUR-DAY SWEET PICKLES

5 qts. (1½ to 3-inch) pickling cucumbers (about 7 lbs.)
½ c. pickling salt
3 c. sugar
3 c. 5% acid strength vinegar
1 tsp. ground turmeric
2 tsp. celery seeds
2 tsp. mixed pickling spices
3 (3-inch) sticks cinnamon
2 c. sugar
2 c. 5% acid strength vinegar
2 c. sugar
1 c. 5% acid strength vinegar

First day: Wash cucumbers; cut ⅛-inch off from each end. Place cucumbers in large container and cover with boiling water. Let stand 6 to 8 hours. Drain. Cover with boiling water.

Second day: Drain; cover with boiling water. Let stand 6 to 8 hours. Drain. Add salt; mix well with cucumbers. Cover with boiling water.

Third day: Drain. Prick each cucumber several times with table fork. Combine 3 c. sugar, 3 c. vinegar, turmeric, celery seeds, pickling spices and cinnamon in large saucepan. Heat to boiling. Pour over cucumbers. (Cucumbers will be partially covered at this point.) Let stand 6 to 8 hours.

Drain syrup into large saucepan. Add 2 c. sugar and 2 c. vinegar to syrup. Heat to boiling; pour over cucumbers.

Fourth day: Drain syrup into large saucepan. Add 2 c. sugar and 1 c. vinegar to syrup. Heat to boiling; pour over pickles. Let stand 6 to 8 hours.

Drain syrup into large saucepan. Add 1 c. sugar. Heat to boiling.

Pack cucumbers into 7 hot, sterilized pint jars. Pour boiling syrup over cucumbers filling to within ¼-inch from the top. Adjust lids.

Process in boiling water bath 5 minutes. Start to count processing time as soon as jars are placed into actively boiling water.

Remove jars. Cool on wire racks 12 to 24 hours. Check jars for airtight seal (see Chapter 1). Makes 7 pints.

FERMENTED DILL PICKLES

20 lbs. (3½ to 5½-inch) pickling cucumbers
½ c. mixed pickling spices
2 to 3 bunches fresh dill
2 c. 5% acid strength vinegar
1½ c. pickling salt
2 gals. water
20 cloves garlic

Cover cucumbers with cold water. Wash thoroughly, using a vegetable brush, handling gently to avoid bruising. Cut ⅛-inch off from each end. Drain on rack or wipe dry.

Place half the pickling spices and a layer of dill in a 5-gal. crock or stone jar. Fill with cucumbers to 3 or 4-inches from top of crock. Mix vinegar, salt and 2 gals. water and pour over the cucumbers. Place a layer of dill and remaining spices over the top of cucumbers. Add 10 cloves garlic.

Cover with a heavy china or glass plate or lid that

fits inside the crock and use a weight, such as a glass jar filled with water on top of the cover to keep cucumbers under the brine. Cover loosely with clean cloth. Keep pickles at room temperature and remove film daily when formed. Film may start forming in 3 to 5 days. Do not stir pickles around in jar but be sure they are completely covered with brine. If necessary, make additional brine, using original proportions.

In about 3 weeks the cucumbers become olive-green and any white spots inside the fermented pickles will be eliminated by processing.

Drain cucumbers. Strain and reserve brine in large saucepan. Bring to boiling. Pack pickles, along with some of the dill, into 10 hot jars. Add 1 clove garlic to each jar. Pour boiling brine over cucumbers, filling to within ¼-inch from the top. Adjust lids.

Process in boiling water bath 15 minutes. Start to count processing time as soon as jars are placed into actively boiling water.

Remove jars. Cool on wire racks 12 to 24 hours. Check jars for airtight seal (see Chapter 1). Makes 9 to 10 quarts.

Note: Use of garlic gives dill pickles the flavor of those sold in delicatessens. The original brine is usually cloudy as a result of yeast development during the fermentation period. If this cloudiness is objectionable, fresh brine may be used to cover the pickles when packing them. Make it with the same proportions of vinegar, salt and water as in the original brine. The fermentation brine is generally preferred for added flavor.

BRINE-CURED PICKLES

Wash cucumbers carefully, taking care not to break the skin. Use freshly harvested, slightly immature pickling variety.

Weigh cucumbers. Put them in a clean, scalded crock or glass container. Cover with a 10% brine solution made by dissolving 1 c. pickling salt in 2 qts. water.

Weight cucumbers down with a scalded plate; place a jar or bag filled with water on top. Be sure cucumbers are covered with brine. Keep at temperature of 68-72°F.

Next day, add 1 c. pickling salt for each 5 pounds of cucumbers. Add salt on top of the plate to prevent its going to the bottom and forming too strong a brine there. (This is necessary to maintain a 10% brine solution.)

Remove scum when it forms on top of the brine. If left on, it will destroy the acidity of the brine and result in spoilage. Check for scum periodically.

At the end of the week and for 4 or 5 succeeding weeks, add ¼ c. pickling salt for each 5 pounds of cucumbers. Add salt as before.

Fermentation resulting in bubble formation should continue about 4 weeks. Test for bubbles by tapping container on the side with your hand. When bubbling ceases, the cucumbers are cured. Add no more salt.

Cucumbers may be stored in this 10% brine solution until made into pickles. Pour a ¼-inch layer of paraffin on top of cucumbers; cover with a lid and continue to store in a cool, dark place (68-72°F).

***Note:** Fresh cucumbers may be added during the first day or two of the curing process if enough brine is added to cover them and if salt is added to maintain 10% brine solution.

TO PICKLE BRINED CUCUMBERS

Brined or cured cucumbers must be desalted before being made into pickles.

Drain cucumbers. Cover cucumbers with hot water (180°F) in crock. Let stand about 4 hours. Stir occasionally.

Lift cucumbers out of water. Pour out water. Rinse container. Return cucumbers to crock; cover with hot water. Let stand 4 hours. Stir occasionally.

Repeat above procedure again. Then drain. Rinse container. Prick cucumbers in several places to prevent shriveling, using table fork. Cover with a weak vinegar solution (1 part water and 3 parts cider vinegar). Let stand 12 hours.

Test to see if sufficient salt has been removed; if not, let stand 12 hours longer. Drain.

Immediately place the "desalted" cucumbers into pickling solution, either for Sour or Sweet Pickles. Both pickles are made with Spiced Vinegar (recipes follow).

SPICED VINEGAR

1 gal. 5% acid strength vinegar
Sugar*
½ oz. whole allspice
½ oz. whole cloves
1 stick cinnamon
1 piece mace

Combine vinegar and sugar in large saucepan. Tie allspice, cloves, cinnamon and mace in cheesecloth bag; add to saucepan. Bring to boiling; simmer 15 minutes.

Cool. Cover and let stand 3 weeks before using.
*Use 2 c. sugar for Sour Pickles and 10 c. for Sweet Pickles (recipes follow).

Sweet Pickles

Pack desalted brined cucumbers in clean crock or glass container.

Heat Spiced Vinegar to boiling (1 pint vinegar for each quart of pickles). Pour boiling liquid over cucumbers. Let stand overnight.

Drain liquid and measure; place in kettle. Add ½ c. sugar for each 2 c. liquid. Bring to boiling; pour over cucumbers. Let stand overnight.

Drain cucumbers; reserve liquid. Add ½ c. sugar for every 2 c. liquid. Heat to boiling.

Pack cucumbers into hot quart jars. Pour boiling liquid over cucumbers, filling to within ¼-inch from the top. Adjust lids.

Process in boiling water bath 15 minutes. Start to count processing time as soon as jars are placed into actively boiling water.

Remove jars. Cool on wire racks 12 to 24 hours. Check jars for airtight seal (see Chapter 1).

Sour Pickles

Use desalted brined pickles. (You will need 1 gal. Spiced Vinegar for each 6 qt. cucumbers.) Place Spiced Vinegar in large kettle. Bring to boiling. Add ¼ of cucumbers at a time. Boil 2 minutes; remove cucumbers. Repeat with remaining cucumbers. Place cucumbers in crock or glass container. Bring Spiced Vinegar to boiling. Pour over cucumbers. Cover crock with thick paper and tie tightly to exclude air. Keep in cool place 6 weeks.

Remove pickles from liquid. Drain liquid into large kettle; bring to boiling. Pack pickles in quart jars. Pour boiling liquid over pickles, filling to within ¼-inch from the top. Adjust lids.

Process in boiling water bath 15 minutes. Start to count processing time as soon as jars are placed into actively boiling water.

Remove jars. Cool on wire racks 12 to 24 hours. Check jars for airtight seal (see Chapter 1).

CHAPTER III

Tangy Vegetables

From the bountiful gardens of late summer come riches for your table—that actually cost a matter of pennies. Colorful, zesty vegetable pickles can lift an everyday meal into the exciting class.

A collection of recipes for good pickled vegetables follows. Among them you'll find familiar friends, such as bright Spiced Carrot Sticks, a timesaver when you're fixing a relish tray, or Pickled Beets for a jiffy salad.

Arrange the Tangy Cauliflower Pickles in your prettiest dish next time you serve a baked ham. Add your own homemade Party Mushroom Pickles to a tossed green salad, or stir a few Sliced Zucchini Pickles in stewed tomatoes for an unusual vegetable course.

Some of our pickles may be new to you. There's peppy Summer Squash Duo made with cubes of tiny yellow crookneck squash and green zucchini, Spiced Pumpkin sealed in a sweet-tart syrup, or Italian Sweet Pepper Slices to brighten up a meat platter.

PICKLED RED CABBAGE

    12 c. shredded red cabbage
    2 c. diced pared tart apple
    3 c. 5% acid strength red wine vinegar
    1⅓ c. brown sugar, firmly packed
    2 tsp. pickling salt
    ½ tsp. caraway seeds
    4 whole cloves

Combine cabbage, apple, vinegar, brown sugar, salt, caraway seeds and cloves in large saucepan. Bring to boiling. Simmer 25 to 30 minutes or until tender-crisp, stirring occasionally. Immediately ladle into 4 hot pint jars, filling to within ¼-inch from the top. Adjust lids.

Process in boiling water bath 15 minutes. Start to count the processing time when water in canner returns to boiling.

Remove jars. Cool on wire racks 12 to 24 hours. Check jars for airtight seal (see Chapter 1). Makes 4 pints.

DILLY GREEN TOMATO SLICES

5 lbs. small, firm green tomatoes
3½ c. 5% acid strength vinegar
3½ c. water
¼ c. pickling salt
4 cloves garlic
¼ c. dill seeds
4 whole cloves
4 bay leaves

Wash and remove stem end from tomatoes. Cut in ¼-inch thick slices.

Combine vinegar, water and salt in large saucepan. Bring to boiling.

Pack tomatoes into 4 hot quart jars. Add 1 clove garlic, 1 tblsp. dill seeds, 1 clove and 1 bay leaf to each jar. Pour boiling liquid over tomatoes, filling to within ¼-inch from the top. Adjust lids.

Process in boiling water bath 15 minutes. Start to count the processing time when water in canner returns to boiling.

Remove jars. Cool on wire racks 12 to 24 hours. Check jars for airtight seal (see Chapter 1). Makes 4 quarts.

GARDEN WALK PICKLES

6 large pickling cucumbers
1 qt. chopped tomatoes
6 medium onions, sliced
4 green peppers, cut in strips
1 c. pickling salt
1 gal. water
1 pt. cut-up small green beans, (1-inch lengths)
1 pt. lima beans
1 lb. carrots, pared and cut in slices
1 pt. cut-up celery (1-inch pieces)
1 medium cauliflower, cut in flowerets
8 c. 5% acid strength white vinegar
7 c. sugar
¼ c. mixed pickling spices
4 tblsp. mustard seeds
2 tblsp. celery seeds

Slice cucumbers, discarding ⅛-inch slice off each end. Combine cucumbers, tomatoes, onions and green peppers in large bowl. Combine salt and water; add to vegetables. Let stand overnight.

Drain vegetables; cover with boiling water. Drain and set aside.

Cook green beans, lima beans, carrots, celery and cauliflower in boiling salted water in large saucepan 20 minutes. Drain and set aside.

Combine vinegar, sugar, pickling spices, mustard seeds and celery seeds in large kettle. Add all vegetables. Bring to boiling; simmer 15 minutes. Immediately ladle into 6 hot, sterilized quart jars, filling to within ¼-inch from the top. Adjust lids.

Process in boiling water bath 5 minutes. Start to

count the processing time when water in canner returns to boiling.

Remove jars. Cool on wire racks 12 to 24 hours. Check jars for airtight seal (see Chapter 1). Makes 6 quarts.

SPICED PUMPKIN

1 (5 lb.) pumpkin, pared, seeded and cut in 1-inch cubes (12 c.)
3 c. sugar
3 c. 5% acid strength white vinegar
1 tblsp. whole allspice
1 tblsp. whole cloves
2 (3-inch) sticks cinnamon

Cook pumpkin in boiling water in large saucepan 6 to 10 minutes or until tender. Drain well.

Combine sugar and vinegar; heat to boiling. Tie allspice, cloves and cinnamon in cheesecloth bag. Add spice bag and pumpkin to boiling liquid. Bring back to boiling; simmer 15 minutes, stirring occasionally. Remove spice bag. Remove pumpkin with slotted spoon and pack into 5 hot, sterilized pint jars. Reheat liquid to boiling; pour immediately over pumpkin, filling to within ¼-inch from the top. Adjust lids.

Process in boiling water bath 10 minutes. Start to count the processing time when water in canner returns to boiling.

Remove jars. Cool on wire racks 12 to 24 hours. Check jars for airtight seal (see Chapter 1). Makes 5 pints.

SPICED CARROT STICKS

5 lbs. medium carrots
3 c. sugar
3½ c. 5% acid strength white vinegar
3 c. water
⅓ c. mustard seeds
1 tblsp. pickling salt
2 (3-inch) cinnamon sticks
12 whole cloves
12 whole allspice

Pare carrots; cut into 4-inch strips. Place in large saucepan with enough salted water to cover. Cook 7 minutes or until tender. Drain.

Combine sugar, vinegar, water, mustard seeds and salt in saucepan. Bring to boiling; simmer 20 minutes.

Pack carrots into 6 hot, sterilized pint jars. Place 1-inch piece cinnamon, 2 whole cloves and 2 allspice in each jar. Pour boiling liquid over carrots, filling to within ¼-inch from the top. Adjust lids.

Process in boiling water bath 10 minutes. Start to count the processing time when water in canner returns to boiling.

Remove jars. Cool on wire racks 12 to 24 hours. Check jars for airtight seal (see Chapter 1). Makes 6 pints.

PICKLED BEETS

24 small beets
1 pt. 5% acid strength vinegar
1¼ c. sugar
2 tblsp. pickling salt
6 whole cloves
1 (3-inch) stick cinnamon
3 medium onions, sliced

Wash beets well. Remove beet tops leaving 1-inch stems and roots. Place in large saucepan and cover with boiling water. Cook, covered, until beets are tender. Drain; reserve 1 c. cooking liquid. Cool beets; remove skins. Cut in slices.

Combine vinegar, sugar, salt and reserved 1 c. liquid in large saucepan. Tie cloves and cinnamon in cheesecloth bag; add to saucepan. Bring to boiling. Add beets and onions; simmer 5 minutes. Remove spice bag. Immediately pack beets and liquid into 4 hot pint jars, filling to within ¼-inch from the top. Adjust lids.

Process in boiling water bath 30 minutes. Start to count the processing time when water in canner returns to boiling.

Remove jars. Cool on wire racks 12 to 24 hours. Check jars for airtight seal (see Chapter 1). Makes 4 pints.

PICKLED ONIONS

    4 qts. small onions
    1 c. pickling salt
    ¼ c. pickling spices
    2 qts. 5% acid strength vinegar
    2 c. sugar

Peel onions; place in bowl. Add salt; let stand overnight.

The next morning, place onions in colander. Rinse thoroughly with cold water to remove all salt. Drain.

Tie pickling spices in cheesecloth bag. Combine vinegar, sugar and spice bag in large kettle. Bring to boiling; boil 10 minutes.

Pack onions into 8 hot, sterilized pint jars. Remove spice bag from boiling liquid. Immediately pour boiling liquid over onions, filling to within ¼-inch from the top. Adjust lids.

Process in boiling water bath 5 minutes. Start to count the processing time when water in canner returns to boiling.

Remove jars. Cool on wire racks 12 to 24 hours. Check jars for airtight seal (see Chapter 1). Makes 8 pints.

PICKLED GREEN BEANS

2½ lbs. green beans
2 large onions, thinly sliced (2 c.)
2 c. sliced celery
2 c. sugar
1 tblsp. mustard seeds
4 tsp. pickling salt
2 tsp. turmeric
2½ c. 5% acid strength white vinegar
1 c. water

Wash beans; cut in 1½-inch slices. Cook beans, onion and celery in boiling water in large saucepan 10 minutes or until tender. Drain well.

Combine sugar, mustard seeds, salt, turmeric, vinegar and water in large saucepan. Bring to boiling. Add vegetables; simmer 5 minutes, stirring occasionally.

Ladle immediately into 6 hot pint jars, filling to within ¼-inch from the top. Adjust lids.

Process in boiling water bath 15 minutes. Start to count the processing time when water in canner returns to boiling.

Remove jars. Cool on wire racks 12 to 24 hours. Check jars for airtight seal (see Chapter 1). Makes 6 pints.

SUMMER SQUASH DUO

1 qt. 5% acid strength cider vinegar
2 c. sugar
¼ c. pickling salt
2 tsp. celery seeds
2 tsp. mustard seeds
2 tsp. ground turmeric
2 lbs. zucchini, cut in ¾-inch chunks
2 lbs. yellow summer squash, cut in ¾-inch chunks
1 qt. sliced onion

Combine vinegar, sugar, salt, celery seeds, mustard seeds and turmeric in kettle. Bring to boiling. Pour boiling liquid over squash and onion in large bowl. Let stand 1 hour.

Return mixture to kettle. Bring to boiling; simmer 3 minutes. Ladle immediately into 6 hot, sterilized pint jars, filling to within ¼-inch from the top. Adjust lids.

Process in boiling water bath 10 minutes. Start to count the processing time when water in canner returns to boiling.

Remove jars. Cool on wire racks 12 to 24 hours. Check jars for airtight seal (see Chapter 1). Makes 6 pints.

TANGY CAULIFLOWER PICKLES

2 medium heads cauliflower, broken in flowerets (2 qts.)
1 c. sliced pared carrots
3 c. 5% acid strength white vinegar
2 c. sugar
¼ c. mustard seeds
4 tsp. celery seeds
⅔ c. chopped sweet red pepper

Cook cauliflower and carrots in boiling salted water in large saucepan 2 minutes. Drain well.

Combine vinegar, sugar, mustard seeds and celery seeds in kettle. Bring to boiling. Add drained vegetables and red pepper; bring to boiling. Immediately ladle into 4 hot pint jars, filling to within ¼-inch from the top. Adjust lids.

Process in boiling water bath 15 minutes. Start to count the processing time when water in canner returns to boiling.

Remove jars. Cool on wire racks 12 to 24 hours. Check jars for airtight seal (see Chapter 1). Makes 4 pints.

PARTY MUSHROOM PICKLES

1 lb. whole fresh mushrooms
2 medium onions
1½ c. 5% acid strength red wine vinegar
1½ c. water
½ c. brown sugar, firmly packed
4 tsp. pickling salt
½ tsp. dried tarragon
½ tsp. dried thyme

Wash mushrooms; trim stems. Thinly slice onions; separate into rings.

Combine onion, vinegar, water, brown sugar, salt, tarragon and thyme in large saucepan. Bring to boiling. Add mushrooms; simmer 5 minutes.

Remove mushrooms and onions from boiling liquid with slotted spoon. Pack into 4 hot, sterilized half-pint jars. Bring liquid back to boiling. Immediately pour over mushrooms, filling to within ¼-inch from the top. Adjust lids.

Process in boiling water bath 10 minutes. Start to count the processing time when water in canner returns to boiling.

Remove jars. Cool on wire racks 12 to 24 hours. Check jars for airtight seals (see Chapter 1). Makes 4 half-pints.

SLICED ZUCCHINI PICKLES

4 qts. thinly sliced unpared zucchini
1 qt. thinly sliced onion
½ c. pickling salt
6 c. 5% acid strength cider vinegar
3 c. sugar
2 tsp. celery seeds
2 tsp. ground turmeric
1 tsp. ground mustard

Combine zucchini, onion and salt. Cover with ice and let stand 3 hours. (If needed, add more ice.) Drain thoroughly.

Combine vinegar, sugar, celery seeds, turmeric and mustard in large saucepan. Bring to boiling. Add drained vegetables; return to boiling. Reduce heat and simmer 3 minutes. Immediately ladle into 6 hot, sterilized pint jars, filling to within ¼-inch from the top. Adjust lids.

Process in boiling water bath 5 minutes. Start to count the processing time when water in canner returns to boiling.

Remove jars. Cool on wire racks 12 to 24 hours. Check for airtight seal (see Chapter 1). Makes 6 pints.

PICKLED BRUSSELS SPROUTS

       3 lbs. Brussels sprouts
       1 lb. small onions
       1¾ c. sugar
       3 tblsp. pickling salt
       2 tblsp. mustard seeds
       2 tsp. celery seeds
       1 qt. 5% acid strength white vinegar
       1⅓ c. water

Wash Brussels sprouts; remove stem and tough outer leaves. Peel onions.

Combine sugar, salt, mustard seeds, celery seeds, vinegar and water in kettle. Heat to boiling. Add vegetables and return to boiling. Reduce heat and simmer 20 minutes or until tender, stirring occasionally. Immediately ladle into 4 hot pint jars, filling to within ¼-inch from the top. Adjust lids.

Process in boiling water bath 15 minutes. Start to count the processing time when water in canner returns to boiling.

Remove jars. Cool on wire racks 12 to 24 hours. Check jars for airtight seal (see Chapter 1). Makes 4 pints.

ITALIAN SWEET PEPPER SLICES

2 lbs. small green peppers
2 lbs. small sweet red peppers
½ c. pickling salt
1 qt. cold water
3 c. 5% acid strength white vinegar
1½ c. water
3 tblsp. sugar
4 tsp. mustard seeds
12 peppercorns

Remove seeds from peppers. Cut in ¼-inch crosswise slices; place in large bowl. Combine salt and water; pour over pepper slices. Let stand 24 hours. Drain and rinse with cold water.

Combine vinegar, water, sugar, mustard seeds and peppercorns in large saucepan. Bring to boiling.

Pack pepper slices in 4 hot, sterilized pint jars. Pour boiling liquid over pepper slices, filling to within ¼-inch from the top. Adjust lids.

Process in boiling water bath 10 minutes. Start to count the processing time when water in canner returns to boiling.

Remove jars. Cool on wire racks 12 to 24 hours. Check jars for airtight seal (see Chapter 1). Makes 4 pints.

CURRIED VEGETABLE PICKLES

1 medium head cauliflower, cut in flowerets
3 large carrots, pared and thinly sliced (2 c.)
12 small onions
6 medium pickling cucumbers
1 qt. 5% acid strength cider vinegar
1½ c. water
2⅔ c. sugar
3 tblsp. pickling salt
2 tblsp. curry powder
1 tblsp. mustard seeds
2 large green peppers, cut in 1-inch squares
2 large sweet red peppers, cut in 1-inch squares
2 c. thinly sliced celery

Cook cauliflower in boiling, salted water in saucepan 1 minute. Drain and set aside.

Cook carrots in boiling, salted water in saucepan 3 minutes. Drain and set aside.

Pour boiling water over onions to cover; let stand 1 minute. Drain and peel off skins.

Cut cucumbers in ¼-inch slices, discarding ⅛-inch slice off each end.

Combine vinegar, water, sugar, salt, curry powder and mustard seeds in large kettle. Add all vegetables. Bring to boiling. Immediately ladle into 6 hot pint jars, filling to within ¼-inch from the top. Adjust lids.

Process in boiling water bath 15 minutes. Start to

count the processing time when water in canner returns to boiling.

Remove jars. Cool on wire racks 12 to 24 hours. Check jars for airtight seal (see Chapter 1). Makes 6 pints.

CABBAGE PICKLES

> 4 lbs. cabbage, shredded (2 medium heads)
> 1½ lbs. onions, chopped (1 qt.)
> 1⅓ c. chopped celery
> ½ c. pickling salt
> 2½ c. sugar
> 6 tblsp. dry mustard
> 1 tblsp. cornstarch
> 1 tblsp. celery seeds
> 1 tblsp. turmeric
> 1½ qts. 5% acid strength white vinegar
> 2 c. water

Combine cabbage, onion, celery and salt in large bowl. Let stand 3 hours. Drain.

Blend together sugar, mustard, cornstarch, celery seeds and turmeric in large kettle. Stir in vinegar and water. Cook, stirring constantly, until mixture comes to boiling. Add drained vegetables; return to boiling. Simmer 15 to 20 minutes or until tender. Immediately ladle into 8 hot pint jars, filling to within ¼-inch from the top. Adjust lids.

Process in boiling water bath 15 minutes. Start to count the processing time when water in canner returns to boiling.

Remove jars. Cool on wire racks 12 to 24 hours. Check jars for airtight seal (see Chapter 1). Makes 8 pints.

CHAPTER IV

Spicy Fruits

Take down the fragrant spices, the sugar canister, and the vinegar bottle. Turn summer's glorious fruits into treats for Christmas giving, for a church bazaar, or to serve around the meat platter to build your reputation as a cook. You'll find your family will gather in the kitchen to enjoy the heavenly aroma of fruits lazily simmering in a spicy pickling syrup.

If your experience with pickling fruits has been limited to spiced peaches, read the recipes that follow and you'll see what you've been missing. Rosy Spiced Pears are really different—it's the cranberry juice that gives them lovely color and flavor. Pickled Red Plums, golden rings of Pineapple Pickles, spicy Pickled Cherries, Curried Apple Wedges or sweet-sour Spiced Green Grapes (wonderful with poultry) could become new favorites.

For a unique dessert, combine sliced oranges with home-canned Spiced Prunes. Or add them to a fruit compote for a new flavor treat.

CURRIED APPLE WEDGES

3 lbs. medium apples, pared
2 qts. water
2 tblsp. 5% acid strength vinegar
1 c. sugar
½ c. light corn syrup
1 c. 5% acid strength vinegar
⅔ c. water
4 tsp. curry powder
4 (3-inch) sticks cinnamon

Core apples; cut into eighths. Place immediately in bowl containing 2 qt. water and 2 tblsp. vinegar.

Combine sugar, corn syrup, vinegar, ⅔ c. water and curry powder in large saucepan. Bring to boiling. Drain apples; add to saucepan. Cover and simmer gently 3 minutes, stirring once or twice.

Remove apples with slotted spoon and pack into 4 hot pint jars. Place 1 stick cinnamon in each jar. Heat syrup back to boiling. Pour boiling syrup over apples, filling to within ¼-inch from the top. Adjust lids.

Process in boiling water bath 15 minutes. Start to count the processing time when water in canner returns to boiling.

Remove jars. Cool on wire racks 12 to 24 hours. Check jars for airtight seal (see Chapter 1). Makes 4 pints.

CALIFORNIA APRICOT PICKLES

4 qts. medium apricots
Whole cloves
4 c. sugar
4 c. brown sugar, firmly packed
1 qt. 5% acid strength vinegar
6 (3-inch) sticks cinnamon

Stud each apricot with 3 cloves.

Combine sugar, brown sugar, vinegar and cinnamon sticks in large kettle. Bring to boiling. Add half of apricots and simmer gently until soft. Remove apricots; add remaining apricots and cook until soft. Remove.

Pack apricots in 6 hot pint jars. Heat syrup to boiling. Remove cinnamon. Pour boiling syrup over apricots, filling to within ¼-inch from the top. Adjust lids.

Process in boiling water bath 20 minutes. Start to count the processing time when water in canner returns to boiling.

Remove jars. Cool on wire racks 12 to 24 hours. Check jars for airtight seal (see Chapter 1). Makes 6 pints.

SPICED BLUEBERRIES

3 qts. fresh blueberries
1 c. 5% acid strength vinegar
1 c. sugar
2 tblsp. whole cloves

Combine blueberries, vinegar and sugar in large saucepan. Tie cloves in cheesecloth bag. Add to saucepan. Bring to boiling. Simmer 20 to 25 minutes or until liquid begins to jell. Pour immediately into 2 hot, sterilized pint jars. Adjust lids.

Process in boiling water bath 5 minutes. Start to count the processing time when water in canner returns to boiling.

Remove jars. Cool on wire racks 12 to 24 hours. Check jars for airtight seal (see Chapter 1). Makes 2 pints.

CANTALOUPE PICKLE

1 medium underripe cantaloupe
1 qt. 5% acid strength vinegar
2 c. water
1 tsp. ground mace
2 (3-inch) sticks cinnamon
2 tblsp. ground cloves
4 c. sugar

Peel cantaloupe and cut in 1-inch cubes. Place in large bowl.

Combine vinegar, water and mace in large kettle. Tie cinnamon and cloves in cheesecloth bag. Add to kettle. Bring to boiling. Immediately pour over cantaloupe. Let stand overnight.

Drain cantaloupe; reserving liquid in large saucepan. Bring to boiling. Stir in sugar. Add cantaloupe; simmer about 1 hour or until cantaloupe is transparent. Remove spice bag.

Remove cantaloupe with slotted spoon and pack into 2 hot, sterilized pint jars. Bring syrup back to boiling. Pour boiling syrup over cantaloupe, filling to within ¼-inch from the top. Adjust lids.

Process in boiling water bath 5 minutes. Start to count the processing time when water in canner returns to boiling.

Remove jars. Cool on wire racks 12 to 24 hours. Check jars for airtight seal (see Chapter 1). Makes 2 pints.

PICKLED CHERRIES

6 lbs. large sweet cherries, stemmed
1 c. sugar
2 c. 5% acid strength white vinegar
½ tsp. ground cinnamon
½ tsp. ground mace
⅛ tsp. ground cloves
8 thin lemon slices

Wash cherries; do not pit.

Combine sugar, vinegar, cinnamon, mace and cloves in large kettle. Bring to boiling. Add cherries; return to boiling. Simmer 1 to 2 minutes or until skins begin to crack. Pour into large bowl. Let stand 4 hours or overnight; stir gently once or twice.

Drain cherries, reserving liquid in saucepan. Bring liquid back to boiling. Pack cherries in 4 hot, sterilized pint jars. Place 2 lemon slices in each jar. Pour boiling liquid over cherries, filling to within ¼-inch from the top. Adjust lids.

Process in boiling water bath 5 minutes. Start to count the processing time when water in canner returns to boiling.

Remove jars. Cool on wire racks 12 to 24 hours. Check jars for airtight seal (see Chapter 1). Makes 4 pints.

SPICED CRANBERRIES

2 (1 lb.) pkgs. fresh cranberries
6 c. sugar
1⅓ c. 5% acid strength vinegar
⅔ c. water
1 tblsp. ground cinnamon
1 tsp. ground cloves
1 tsp. ground allspice

Combine cranberries, sugar, vinegar, water, cinnamon, cloves and allspice in large saucepan. Boil gently, stirring occasionally, for 40 minutes or until mixture thickens.

Immediately ladle into 2 hot, sterilized pint jars, filling to within ¼-inch from the top. Adjust lids.

Process in boiling water bath 5 minutes. Start to count the processing time when water in canner returns to boiling.

Remove jars. Cool on wire racks 12 to 24 hours. Check jars for airtight seal (see Chapter 1). Makes 2 pints.

SPICED GREEN GRAPES

2 lbs. green seedless grapes, stemmed
1 c. sugar
2 c. 5% acid strength white vinegar
1 tsp. whole cloves
1 (3-inch) stick cinnamon

Wash grapes.

Combine sugar and vinegar in saucepan. Tie cloves and cinnamon in cheesecloth bag and add to saucepan. Bring to boiling. Reduce heat and simmer 5 minutes. Add grapes and return to boiling. Simmer slowly 1 to 2 minutes or until tender. Remove spice bag.

Remove grapes with slotted spoon and pack into 2 hot, sterilized pint jars. Bring syrup back to boiling. Pour boiling syrup over grapes, filling to within ¼-inch from the top. Adjust lids.

Process in boiling water bath 5 minutes. Start to count the processing time when water in canner returns to boiling.

Remove jars. Cool on wire rack 12 to 24 hours. Check jars for airtight seal (see Chapter 1). Makes 2 pints.

PEACH PICKLES

    4 lbs. peaches (about 16 medium)
    1 tblsp. whole cloves
    2 qts. water
    2 tblsp. 5% acid strength vinegar
    4 c. sugar
    1½ c. 5% acid strength vinegar
    ¾ c. water
    1 (1-inch) piece fresh ginger root
    2 (3-inch) sticks cinnamon

Wash peaches; place in large container. Pour boiling water over peaches; let stand until skins slip off easily when dipped in cold water. Stud each peach with a clove and place in large bowl containing 2 qt. water and 2 tblsp. vinegar.

Combine sugar, 1½ c. vinegar and ¾ c. water in large kettle. Tie ginger root, remaining cloves and cinnamon in cheesecloth bag. Add to saucepan. Bring to boiling. Drain peaches; add to saucepan. Cover and simmer 10 minutes or until tender. Pour mixture into large container. Let stand overnight.

Drain peaches; reserve syrup in saucepan. Remove spice bag. Bring syrup back to boiling. Pack peaches in 4 hot pint jars, filling to within ¼-inch from the top. Adjust lids.

Process in boiling water bath 20 minutes. Start to count the processing time when water in canner returns to boiling.

Remove jars. Cool on wire rack 12 to 24 hours. Check jars for airtight seal (see Chapter 1). Makes 4 pints.

PICKLED PEACH HALVES

    2 lbs. medium peaches
    1 qt. water
    ½ tsp. Fruit-fresh
    2 c. sugar
    1 c. 5% acid strength white vinegar
    2 tblsp. chopped crystallized ginger
    2 (3-inch) sticks cinnamon
    8 whole blanched almonds

Wash peaches; place in large container. Pour boiling water over peaches; let stand until skin slips off easily when dipped in cold water. Place peaches into bowl containing 1 qt. water and Fruit-fresh. Halve and pit peaches.

Combine sugar and vinegar in saucepan. Tie ginger and cinnamon in cheesecloth bag; add to saucepan. Bring to boiling; boil 5 minutes. Drain peaches; add to syrup. Simmer 5 minutes. Remove peaches with slotted spoon and pack into 2 hot pint jars. Place 4 almonds in each jar. Remove spice bag from syrup. Bring syrup back to boiling. Pour boiling syrup over peaches, filling to within ¼-inch from the top. Adjust lids.

Process in boiling water bath 20 minutes. Start to count the processing time when water in canner returns to boiling.

Remove jars. Cool on wire rack 12 to 24 hours. Check jars for airtight seal (see Chapter 1). Makes 2 pints.

PEACH AND APRICOT PICKLES

4 lbs. medium peaches, pared and halved
Whole cloves
1½ lbs. apricots
4 (3-inch) sticks cinnamon
2½ c. sugar
2 c. 5% acid strength white vinegar

Place peaches in large kettle. Cover with boiling water. Heat over high heat 3 minutes to scald. Drain peaches, reserving 1 cup cooking liquid.

Stick 1 clove in each peach half and 1 clove in each apricot. Combine 1 c. reserved liquid, cinnamon sticks, apricots, sugar and vinegar in large kettle. Bring to boiling; simmer 5 minutes. Combine mixture with peaches in large container. Let stand 4 hours or overnight. Remove cinnamon.

Pack peaches and apricots in 6 hot pint jars. Heat syrup in saucepan to boiling. Pour boiling syrup over fruit, filling to within ¼-inch from the top. Adjust lids.

Process in boiling water bath 15 minutes. Start to count the processing time when water in canner returns to boiling.

Remove jars. Cool on wire racks 12 to 24 hours. Check jars for airtight seal (see Chapter 1). Makes 6 pints.

PEAR PICKLES

3½ lbs. ripe pears (about 14 to 16 medium)
1 qt. water
1 tblsp. 5% acid strength vinegar
2½ c. sugar
1¼ c. 5% acid strength vinegar
1 c. water
1 (2-inch) piece fresh ginger root
2 tblsp. whole cloves
7 (3-inch) sticks cinnamon

Wash pears. Pare, halve and core pears. Place in large bowl containing 1 qt. water and 1 tblsp. vinegar.

Combine sugar, 1¼ c. vinegar and 1 c. water in saucepan. Tie ginger, cloves and cinnamon in cheesecloth bag; add to saucepan. Bring to boiling. Cover; boil 5 minutes.

Drain pears. Pack pears into 3 hot pint jars. Remove spice bag from syrup. Bring syrup back to boiling. Pour boiling syrup over pears, filling to within ¼-inch from the top. Adjust lids.

Process in boiling water bath 15 minutes. Start to count the processing time when water in canner returns to boiling.

Remove jars. Cool on wire racks 12 to 24 hours. Check jars for airtight seal (see Chapter 1). Makes 3 pints.

ROSY SPICED PEARS

1 (32 oz.) bottle cranberry/apple
 juice cocktail
1½ c. honey
1 c. 5% acid strength wine vinegar
3 (3-inch) sticks cinnamon
½ tsp. whole cloves
½ tsp. red food coloring
6 lbs. firm, almost ripe pears, pared,
 halved and cored

Combine cranberry/apple juice, honey, vinegar, cinnamon sticks, cloves and food coloring. Bring to boiling. Reduce heat and simmer 5 minutes. Add half of pears; simmer 2 minutes. Remove pears. Repeat with remaining pears. Bring syrup back to boiling.

Pack pears in 6 hot pint jars. Pour boiling syrup over pears, filling to within ¼-inch from the top. Adjust lids.

Process in boiling water bath 15 minutes. Start to count the processing time when water in canner returns to boiling.

Remove jars. Cool on wire racks 12 to 24 hours. Check jars for airtight seal (see Chapter 1). Makes 6 pints.

PINEAPPLE PICKLES

2 medium pineapples
1½ c. sugar
¾ c. water
⅓ c. 5% acid strength vinegar
10 whole cloves
1 (3-inch) stick cinnamon

Cut pineapple in ¼-inch crosswise slices; peel and remove eyes. Cut slices into quarters; remove cores.

Combine sugar, water, vinegar, cloves and cinnamon in large saucepan. Add pineapple; simmer 30 minutes. Immediately ladle pineapple and syrup into 2 hot pint jars, filling to within ¼-inch from the top. Adjust lids.

Process in boiling water bath 20 minutes. Start to count the processing time when water in canner returns to boiling.

Remove jars. Cool on wire racks 12 to 24 hours. Check jars for airtight seal (see Chapter 1). Makes 2 pints.

SPICED PRUNES

2 (12 oz.) pkgs. pitted prunes
1½ qts. water
2⅔ c. brown sugar, firmly packed
3⅓ c. 5% acid strength cider vinegar
6 (3-inch) sticks cinnamon
4 tsp. whole allspice
2 tsp. whole cloves

Combine prunes and water in large saucepan. Bring to a boil. Reduce heat and simmer 3 minutes or until prunes are tender. Drain.

Combine brown sugar and vinegar in large saucepan. Tie cinnamon, allspice and cloves in cheesecloth bag; add to saucepan. Bring to boiling. Reduce heat and simmer 5 minutes. Add prunes and continue simmering 5 minutes.

Remove prunes with slotted spoon and pack in 3 hot pint jars. Bring syrup back to boiling; remove spice bag. Pour boiling syrup over prunes, filling to within ¼-inch from the top. Adjust lids.

Process in boiling water bath 15 minutes. Start to count the processing time when water in canner returns to boiling.

Remove jars. Cool on wire racks 12 to 24 hours. Check jars for airtight seals (see Chapter 1). Makes 3 pints.

PICKLED RED PLUMS

3½ lbs. red plums, Santa Rosa type (3 qts.)
1½ c. sugar
1 c. brown sugar, firmly packed
2 c. 5% acid strength vinegar
3 (3-inch) sticks cinnamon
1½ tsp. whole cloves

Wash plums; prick skins with needle. (This helps prevent fruit from bursting).

Combine sugar, brown sugar and vinegar in large kettle. Tie cinnamon and cloves in cheesecloth bag; add to kettle. Bring to boiling.

Add half the plums and simmer gently 7 to 8 minutes or until soft. Remove fruit with slotted spoon. Add remaining fruit; simmer 7 to 8 minutes. Remove plums with slotted spoon and pack all the plums into 5 hot pint jars. Heat syrup back to boiling. Pour boiling syrup over plums, filling to within ¼-inch from the top. Adjust lids.

Process in boiling water bath 15 minutes. Start to count the processing time when water in canner returns to boiling.

Remove jars. Cool on wire racks 12 to 24 hours. Check jars for airtight seal (see Chapter 1). Makes 5 pints.

WATERMELON PICKLES

Rind of 1 (20 lb.) watermelon
1 gal. cold water
2 tblsp. pickling salt
2 c. 5% acid strength vinegar
7 c. sugar
1 tblsp. whole cloves
2 or 3 sticks cinnamon

Choose a melon with thick, firm rind. Trim off outer green skin and pink flesh, leaving a very thin line of pink. Stamp out rind with small cookie cutter or cut into neat squares. Place in large container.

Combine 1 gal. cold water and 2 tblsp. salt; add to watermelon rind. Let stand overnight. Drain; rinse with cold water. Cover with ice water; let stand 1 hour.

Drain. Place in large kettle. Cover rind with boiling water. Bring to boiling; reduce heat and simmer until tender. Drain well.

Combine vinegar and sugar in large kettle. Tie cloves and cinnamon sticks in cheesecloth bag; add to kettle. Bring to boiling. Add rind. Cook gently until rind is clear and transparent. Remove spice bag. Turn rind and syrup into a crock and let stand 24 hours.

Drain rind; reserve syrup in large saucepan. Bring to boiling. Pack rind in 6 hot, sterilized pint jars. Pour boiling syrup over rind, filling to within ¼-inch from the top. Adjust lids.

Process in boiling water bath 5 minutes. Start to count the processing time when water in canner returns to boiling.

Remove jars. Cool on wire racks 12 to 24 hours. Check jars for airtight seal (see Chapter 1). Makes 6 pints.

CHAPTER V

Piquant Relishes

Whether it's a family supper on a brisk winter night, a bring-a-dish church or club gathering, or a company buffet, you can count on flavorful relishes to give that extra zip and flair. We have a colorful collection of vegetable relishes to choose from. Serve an assortment on a relish tray, or use them in sandwich spreads and salad dressings. Youngsters enjoy their favorite sandwiches even more with Mom's homemade hot dog or hamburger relishes.

Nothing adds appetite appeal more quickly and easily to chicken or pork dinners than Corn/Tomato Relish with its mingling of yellow kernels, bits of tomato and red and green pepper in a pickling mixture. Save busy holiday time by opening a jar of tantalizing Cranberry/Orange Relish while you're fixing the turkey dinner. Our trio of Chutneys—Peach, Tomato/Apple and Mint are just right with curried rice. For a fall treat, spoon one of these homemade chutneys into baked acorn squash.

COUNTRY CARROT RELISH

6 large carrots (1 lb.)
4 pickling cucumbers (1 lb.)
2 medium onions
1 large green pepper
2 tblsp. pickling salt
1¾ c. sugar
2⅓ c. 5% acid strength cider vinegar
2 tsp. celery seeds
1 tsp. mustard seeds

Coarsely grind carrots, cucumbers, onions and green pepper; place in large bowl. Stir in salt. Let stand 3 hours; drain.

Combine sugar, vinegar, celery seeds and mustard seeds in large kettle. Bring to boiling. Add vegetables. Return to boiling. Reduce heat and simmer 20 minutes, stirring occasionally. Immediately ladle into 7 hot half-pint jars, filling to within ¼-inch from the top. Adjust lids.

Process in boiling water bath 15 minutes. Start to count the processing time when water in canner returns to boiling.

Remove jars. Cool on wire racks 12 to 24 hours. Check jars for airtight seal (see Chapter 1). Makes 7 half-pints.

ZUCCHINI HASH

2 lbs. zucchini (4 to 6 small)
2 lbs. onions (8 medium)
1 lb. carrots (6 to 8)
3 large green peppers
¾ c. sugar
¼ c. pickling salt
1 tblsp. celery seeds
1 tsp. mustard seeds
2¼ c. 5% acid strength vinegar
½ c. water

Coarsely grind zucchini, onions, carrots and green peppers. Place in large kettle. Add sugar, salt, celery seeds, mustard seeds, vinegar and water. Bring to boiling. Reduce heat and simmer 20 minutes, stirring frequently. Immediately ladle into 6 hot pint jars, filling to within ¼-inch from the top. Adjust lids.

Process in boiling water bath 15 minutes. Start to count the processing time when water in canner returns to boiling.

Remove jars. Cool on wire racks 12 to 24 hours. Check jars for airtight seal (see Chapter 1). Makes 6 pints.

PEPPY CELERY RELISH

2 c. 5% acid strength white vinegar
½ c. water
1¼ c. sugar
2 tblsp. pickling salt
2 tblsp. mustard seeds
1 tsp. ground turmeric
2 qts. chopped celery (2 lbs.)
3 c. chopped onion (4 to 5 medium)
1½ c. chopped green pepper (2 to 3)
1½ c. chopped sweet red pepper (2 to 3)

Combine vinegar, water, sugar, salt, mustard seeds and turmeric in large kettle. Bring to boiling. Add celery, onion, green pepper and red pepper. Return mixture to boiling. Simmer 10 minutes. Immediately ladle into 6 hot pint jars, filling to within ¼-inch from the top. Adjust lids.

Process in boiling water bath 15 minutes. Start to count the processing time when water in canner returns to boiling.

Remove jars. Cool on wire racks 12 to 24 hours. Check jars for airtight seal (see Chapter 1). Makes 6 pints.

EGGPLANT RELISH

2 large eggplants (1½ lbs. each)
5 large tomatoes, peeled
3 green peppers, seeded
2 onions, peeled and quartered
2 cloves garlic, minced
1 c. 5% acid strength vinegar
½ c. salad oil
2 tblsp. pickling salt
½ tsp. pepper

Bake eggplant in 400° oven until soft, about 30 minutes. Peel and cut up. Put eggplant, tomatoes, peppers and onions through food grinder, using medium blade.

Combine ground vegetables, garlic, vinegar, oil, salt and pepper in large kettle. Bring to boiling. Reduce heat and simmer 20 minutes or until the consistency of a chutney. Immediately ladle into 10 hot half-pint jars, filling to within ¼-inch from the top. Adjust lids.

Process in boiling water bath 30 minutes. Start to count the processing time when water in canner returns to boiling.

Remove jars. Cool on racks 12 to 24 hours. Check jars for airtight seal (see Chapter 1). Makes 10 half-pints.

SWEET CORN RELISH

10 c. fresh, frozen or canned whole kernel corn
7 c. shredded cabbage
2 c. chopped onion
¾ c. chopped green pepper
¾ c. chopped sweet red pepper
2 tblsp. dry mustard
1½ tsp. flour
½ tsp. ground turmeric
4 c. 5% acid strength cider vinegar
2 c. sugar
2 tblsp. pickling salt

Combine corn, cabbage, onion, green and red pepper in large kettle.

Mix together mustard, flour and turmeric. Add ¼ c. vinegar to mustard mixture; stir to blend well. Add mustard mixture, remaining vinegar, sugar and salt to vegetables, mixing well. Bring to boiling; simmer 15 minutes. Immediately ladle into 8 hot pint jars, filling to within ¼-inch from the top. Adjust lids.

Process in boiling water bath 15 minutes. Start to count the processing time when water in canner returns to boiling.

Remove jars. Cool on wire racks 12 to 24 hours. Check jars for airtight seal (see Chapter 1). Makes 8 pints.

CORN/TOMATO RELISH

4 c. corn cut from cob (about 6 ears)
2 c. chopped, peeled tomatoes (4 medium)
2 c. chopped onion
2 c. chopped green pepper (4 medium)
1 c. chopped celery
1 c. 5% acid strength vinegar
½ c. sugar
2 tblsp. pickling salt
1 tblsp. ground turmeric
2 tsp. mustard seeds
2 tblsp. cornstarch
¼ c. water

Combine corn, tomatoes, onion, green pepper, celery, vinegar, sugar, salt, turmeric and mustard seeds in large kettle. Bring to boiling. Reduce heat and simmer 10 minutes, stirring occasionally.

Blend together cornstarch and water; add to vegetables. Return to boiling; cook, stirring constantly, 2 to 3 minutes. Immediately ladle into 5 hot pint jars, filling to within ¼-inch from the top. Adjust lids.

Process in boiling water bath 15 minutes. Start to count the processing time when water in canner returns to boiling.

Remove jars. Cool on wire racks 12 to 24 hours. Check jars for airtight seal (see Chapter 1). Makes 5 pints.

GOLDEN GLOW RELISH

2 qts. pared and seeded pickling cucumbers (cut in 2-inch cubes)
2½ c. ground carrots
2 c. ground onion
1 c. ground sweet red peppers
1½ c. ground green peppers
1 (4 oz.) jar pimiento, chopped
3 c. water
2 tblsp. pickling salt
3 c. 5% acid strength cider vinegar
2 c. sugar
1 tsp. dry mustard
½ tsp. ground turmeric

Grind cucumbers; combine with carrots, onion, red and green pepper, pimiento, water and salt in large bowl. Let stand 3 hours. Drain off brine.

Combine vegetables, vinegar, sugar, mustard and turmeric in large saucepan. Bring to boiling; simmer 10 minutes. Ladle into 6 hot, sterilized pint jars, filling to within ¼-inch from the top. Adjust lids.

Process in boiling water bath 10 minutes. Start to count the processing time when water in canner returns to boiling.

Remove jars. Cool on wire racks 12 to 24 hours. Check jars for airtight seal (see Chapter 1). Makes 6 pints.

MIXED VEGETABLE RELISH

       3 c. finely chopped carrots
       1½ c. finely chopped onion
       1 c. finely chopped green pepper
       1 c. finely chopped cabbage
       2 c. 5% acid strength cider vinegar
       1 c. light corn syrup
       1½ tblsp. pickling salt
       1½ tsp. mustard seeds
       1½ tsp. celery seeds
       ¼ c. diced pimiento

Combine carrots, onion, green pepper and cabbage in large bowl. Cover vegetables with boiling water. Let stand 5 minutes. Drain well.

Combine vegetables, vinegar, corn syrup, salt, mustard seeds and celery seeds in large saucepan. Bring to a boil, stirring constantly. Reduce heat and simmer, stirring occasionally, 25 minutes or until mixture thickens. Add pimiento during the last 5 minutes of cooking time. Ladle into 5 hot, sterilized half-pint jars, filling to within ¼-inch from top. Adjust lids.

Process in boiling water bath 10 minutes. Start to count the processing time when water in canner returns to boiling.

Remove jars. Cool on wire racks 12 to 24 hours. Check jars for airtight seal (see Chapter 1). Makes 5 half-pints.

BEET AND HORSERADISH RELISH

4 c. ground cooked beets
1 c. prepared hot horseradish
1 c. 5% acid strength vinegar
¾ c. sugar
1½ tsp. pickling salt
½ tsp. paprika

Combine beets, horseradish, vinegar, sugar, salt and paprika in large saucepan. Heat to boiling. Immediately ladle into 6 hot, sterilized half-pint jars, filling to within ¼-inch from the top. Adjust lids.

Process in boiling water bath 5 minutes. Start to count the processing time when water in canner returns to boiling.

Remove jars. Cool on wire racks 12 to 24 hours. Check jars for airtight seal (see Chapter 1). Makes 6 half-pints.

RIPE CUCUMBER RELISH

12 large ripe yellow pickling cucumbers
12 onions (2-inches in diameter)
¾ c. pickling salt
1 qt. 5% acid strength vinegar
4 c. sugar
2 tblsp. mustard seeds
2 large stalks celery, diced
6 large green peppers, diced

Peel cucumbers, scoop out and discard seeds and center; dice pulp into ¼-inch cubes. Dice onions in ¼-inch cubes. Place cucumbers, onion and salt in large bowl. Cover and let stand 10 to 12 hours. Drain through white cloth until dry.

Combine vinegar, sugar and mustard seeds in large kettle; add drained vegetables, celery and green pepper. Cook over low heat until the mixture is thick and the cucumbers are golden in color. Ladle into 6 hot sterilized pint jars, filling to within ¼-inch from the top. Adjust lids.

Process in boiling water bath 5 minutes. Start to count the processing time when water in canner returns to boiling.

Remove jars. Cool on wire racks 12 to 24 hours. Check jars for airtight seal (see Chapter 1). Makes 6 pints.

ONION HAMBURGER RELISH

4 lbs. large white onions (about 12)
1 tblsp. pickling salt
2 unpared green apples
2 sweet red peppers
1½ c. 5% acid strength cider vinegar
1½ c. sugar
2 tsp. mustard seeds
1 tsp. celery seeds
1 tsp. white pepper

Put onions through food grinder, using a medium blade. Place in bowl; mix in salt. Let stand overnight. Press out liquid through a strainer.

Core apples; seed peppers. Chop finely. Combine drained onion, apples, peppers, vinegar, sugar, mustard seeds, celery seeds and pepper in large kettle. Bring to boiling. Reduce heat and simmer 10 minutes. Immediately ladle into 4 hot pint jars, filling to within ¼-inch from the top. Adjust lids.

Process in boiling water bath 15 minutes. Start to count the processing time when water in canner returns to boiling.

Remove jars. Cool on wire racks 12 to 24 hours. Check jars for airtight seal (see Chapter 1). Makes 4 pints.

HOT DOG RELISH

⅔ c. sugar
2 tblsp. flour
4 tsp. pickling salt
1 c. 5% acid strength cider vinegar
⅔ c. water
½ c. French-style prepared mustard
6 c. finely chopped pickling cucumbers (6 to 8 medium)
1 c. finely chopped onion (1 large)
2 c. finely chopped sweet red pepper (2 large)

Blend together sugar, flour and salt in large kettle. Gradually stir in vinegar, water and mustard. Cook, stirring constantly, until mixture comes to a boil. Stir in cucumbers, onion and pepper. Return to boiling; simmer 5 minutes. Immediately ladle into 4 hot pint jars, filling to within ¼-inch from the top. Adjust lids.

Process in boiling water bath 15 minutes. Start to count the processing time when water in canner returns to boiling.

Remove jars. Cool on wire racks 12 to 24 hours. Check jars for airtight seal (see Chapter 1). Makes 4 pints.

BEST-EVER PICCALILLI

22 medium green tomatoes, quartered
1 pt. small onions
6 green peppers, quartered
6 sweet red peppers, quartered
1 qt. 5% acid strength vinegar
1 pt. 5% acid strength vinegar
3½ c. sugar
¼ c. pickling salt
1½ tsp. ground allspice
1½ tsp. ground cinnamon
4 tsp. celery seeds
½ c. mustard seeds

Put tomatoes, onions and peppers through food chopper, using medium blade. Drain.

Place vegetables in large kettle; add 1 qt. vinegar. Boil 30 minutes, stirring frequently. Drain and discard liquid. Return vegetables to kettle and add remaining 1 pt. vinegar, sugar, salt, allspice, cinnamon, celery seeds and mustard seeds. Simmer 3 minutes. Immediately ladle into 6 hot, sterilized pint jars, filling to within ¼-inch from the top. Adjust lids.

Process in boiling water bath 5 minutes. Start to count the processing time when water in canner returns to boiling.

Remove jars. Cool on wire racks 12 to 24 hours. Check jars for airtight seal (see Chapter 1). Makes 6 pints.

CHOWCHOW

1 medium head cabbage, chopped (2 qts.)
6 medium onions, chopped
6 green peppers, coarsely chopped
6 sweet red peppers, coarsely chopped
1 qt. chopped green tomatoes
¼ c. pickling salt
2 tblsp. prepared mustard
6 c. 5% acid strength vinegar
2½ c. sugar
1½ tsp. ground turmeric
1 tsp. ground ginger
2 tblsp. mustard seeds
1 tblsp. mixed pickling spices

Combine cabbage, onion, peppers, tomatoes and salt in large bowl. Cover; let stand overnight. Drain.

Mix mustard with a little vinegar in kettle; add remaining vinegar, sugar, turmeric, ginger, mustard seeds and pickling spices. Simmer 20 minutes. Add vegetables; simmer 10 minutes. Immediately ladle into 7 hot, sterilized pint jars, filling to within ¼-inch from the top. Adjust lids.

Process in boiling water bath 5 minutes. Start to count the processing time when water in canner returns to boiling.

Remove jars. Cool on wire racks 12 to 24 hours. Check jars for airtight seal (see Chapter 1). Makes 7 pints.

APPLE CHOWCHOW

      6 c. pared, chopped apple
      4 c. chopped celery
      2 c. chopped carrots
      1⅓ c. chopped green pepper
      1⅓ c. chopped sweet red pepper
      3 tblsp. pickling salt
      2½ c. sugar
      1 tsp. ground turmeric
      1 tsp. mustard seeds
      3⅓ c. 5% acid strength cider vinegar

Combine apple, celery, carrots, green and red peppers and salt in large bowl. Let stand 4 to 6 hours; drain well.

Combine sugar, turmeric, mustard seeds and vinegar in large kettle. Bring to boiling. Add vegetables. Return to boiling. Reduce heat and simmer 15 minutes. Immediately ladle into 5 hot pint jars, filling to within ¼-inch from the top. Adjust lids.

Process in boiling water bath 15 minutes. Start to count the processing time when water in canner returns to boiling.

Remove jars. Cool on wire racks 12 to 24 hours. Check jars for airtight seal (see Chapter 1). Makes 5 pints.

FISH FRY CHOWCHOW

5 lbs. pickling cucumbers (6 large)
6 medium onions
¼ c. pickling salt
2 tblsp. prepared mustard
4 tsp. ground turmeric
4 tsp. cornstarch
2½ c. 5% acid strength white vinegar
1 c. dark brown sugar, firmly packed
1 c. light brown sugar, firmly packed
1 (4 oz.) jar pimiento, drained and chopped
1 medium green pepper, chopped

Peel and cut cucumbers in ¼-inch slices. Slice onions thinly. Place in large bowl and sprinkle with salt. Cover; refrigerate overnight.

Drain off any liquid. Chop cucumbers and onions.

Blend together mustard, turmeric and cornstarch. Add enough vinegar to make a thin paste. Combine paste, remaining vinegar and brown sugars in large kettle. Bring to boiling, stirring frequently. Add cucumbers and onions; bring to full rolling boil. Add pimiento and green pepper.

Immediately ladle into 5 hot, sterilized pint jars, filling to within ¼-inch from the top. Adjust lids.

Process in boiling water bath 5 minutes. Start to count the processing time when water in canner returns to boiling.

Remove jars. Cool on wire racks 12 to 24 hours. Check jars for airtight seal (see Chapter 1). Makes 5 pints.

CRANBERRY/ORANGE RELISH

1 lb. cranberries (4 c.)
1 medium orange
1 c. raisins
1 c. 5% acid strength cider vinegar
1 (6 oz.) can frozen orange juice concentrate
2 c. sugar
¼ tsp. ground cinnamon
¼ tsp. ground cloves

Coarsely chop cranberries; place in large kettle. Remove thin outer peel from orange; cut peel into slivers and add to cranberries. Remove white membrane from orange. Cut orange into segments.

Stir in orange segments, raisins, vinegar, orange concentrate, sugar, cinnamon and cloves. Bring to boiling. Reduce heat and simmer 15 minutes or until mixture thickens. Immediately ladle into 5 hot, sterilized half-pint jars, filling to within ¼-inch from the top. Adjust lids.

Process in boiling water bath 10 minutes. Start to count the processing time when water in canner returns to boiling.

Remove jars. Cool on racks 12 to 24 hours. Check jars for airtight seal (see Chapter 1). Makes 5 half-pints.

PEACH CHUTNEY

4 qts. chopped pared peaches
1 c. chopped onion
1 clove garlic, minced
1 hot pepper
1 c. raisins
1 qt. 5% acid strength vinegar
2 tblsp. ground ginger
¼ c. mustard seeds
3 c. brown sugar, firmly packed
2 tsp. pickling salt

Combine peaches, onion, garlic, hot pepper, raisins, vinegar, ginger, mustard seeds, brown sugar and salt in large kettle. Bring to boiling; reduce heat and simmer until thickened. Remove hot pepper. Immediately ladle into 8 hot, sterilized pint jars, filling to within ¼-inch from the top. Adjust lids.

Process in boiling water bath 5 minutes. Start to count the processing time when water in canner returns to boiling.

Remove jars. Cool on wire racks 12 to 24 hours. Check jars for airtight seal (see Chapter 1). Makes 8 pints.

MINT CHUTNEY

2 c. chopped, peeled tomatoes (1 lb.)
2 c. chopped tart apples (1 lb.)
1⅓ c. chopped green pepper
1½ c. chopped onion
1½ c. raisins
½ c. chopped fresh mint leaves
2 tsp. dry mustard
2 tsp. pickling salt
3 c. brown sugar, firmly packed
3 c. 5% acid strength cider vinegar

Combine tomatoes, apples, green pepper, onion, raisins, mint, mustard, salt, brown sugar and vinegar in large kettle. Bring to boiling. Simmer 50 to 60 minutes or until thickened, stirring frequently. Immediately ladle into 6 hot half-pint jars, filling to within ¼-inch from the top. Adjust lids.

Process in boiling water bath 15 minutes. Start to count the processing time when water in canner returns to boiling.

Remove jars. Cool on racks 12 to 24 hours. Check jars for airtight seal (see Chapter 1). Makes 6 half-pints.

TOMATO/APPLE CHUTNEY

5 lbs. ripe tomatoes, peeled and diced (10 c.)
3 lbs. tart apples, pared and diced (6 c.)
2 large onions, chopped (2 c.)
1 (15 oz.) pkg. raisins
2 cloves garlic, minced
1 lb. brown sugar
1 tblsp. pickling salt
1 tblsp. ground cinnamon
2 tsp. crushed dried red peppers
2 tsp. mustard seeds
1 tsp. ground allspice
½ tsp. ground ginger
½ tsp. ground cloves
2 c. 5% acid strength cider vinegar

Combine tomatoes, apples, onion, raisins, garlic, brown sugar, salt, cinnamon, peppers, mustard seeds, allspice, ginger, cloves and vinegar in large kettle. Bring to boiling, stirring constantly. Cover; simmer 10 minutes. Uncover and continue simmering 20 to 30 minutes or until thick, stirring frequently. Immediately ladle into 12 hot half-pint jars, filling to within ¼-inch from the top. Adjust lids.

Process in boiling water bath 15 minutes. Start to count the processing time when water in canner returns to boiling.

Remove jars. Cool on racks 12 to 24 hours. Check jars for airtight seal (see Chapter 1). Makes 12 half-pints.

GREEN TOMATO/PEPPER MELANGE

2 qts. cored, chopped green tomatoes (4 lbs.)
1½ c. chopped green pepper (2 large)
1 c. chopped onion (1 large)
⅔ c. chopped sweet red pepper (1 large)
¼ c. pickling salt
1½ c. 5% acid strength cider vinegar
½ c. water
1 c. sugar
½ tsp. mixed pickling spices

Combine tomatoes, green pepper, onion, red pepper and salt in large bowl. Cover and let stand overnight. Drain well.

Combine vinegar, water and sugar in large kettle. Tie pickling spices in cheesecloth bag; add to kettle. Bring to boiling. Add vegetables; return to boiling. Simmer 30 minutes, stirring occasionally. Immediately ladle into 3 hot pint jars, filling to within ¼-inch from the top. Adjust lids.

Process in boiling water bath 15 minutes. Start to count the processing time when water in canner returns to boiling.

Remove jars. Cool on wire racks 12 to 24 hours. Check jars for airtight seal (see Chapter 1). Makes 3 pints.

CHAPTER VI

Peppy Sauces

Jars of homemade sauces will save you both time and money when you're fixing meats, poultry or fish—and add that extra something to familiar dishes.

The recipes that follow make superior sauces. Classic examples are Barbecue Sauce for indoor and outdoor cooking and spicy Taco Sauce for a quick Mexican meal. For chili sauce lovers, there are a number of sauces to choose from—mild or hot to please every taste. And if frost threatens and you're wondering what to do with the green tomatoes, salvage some of them in spicy Green Tomato Chili Sauce.

Plum Ketchup, one of the most unusual, is a company special alongside a platter of ham or pork. We offer several other different and delicious fruit ketchups to brighten an everyday meal.

Looking for an outstanding gift? Wrap a jar of cranberry, plum or grape ketchup in bright-colored tissue paper—the recipient will be delighted wth this out-of-the-ordinary homemade gift. Gourmet, yet inexpensive, because you made it yourself.

HOT CHILI SAUCE

5 lbs. tomatoes, peeled and chopped (2 qts.)
1 large onion, chopped (1 c.)
1 large green pepper, chopped (¾ c.)
¾ c. sugar
1¼ c. 5% acid strength cider vinegar
1 tblsp. pickling salt
1 tsp. crushed red pepper
1 tsp. mustard seeds
½ tsp. ground ginger
½ tsp. ground nutmeg
¼ tsp. ground cloves

Combine tomatoes, onion, green pepper, sugar, vinegar, salt, red pepper, mustard seeds, ginger, nutmeg and cloves in large kettle. Bring to boiling. Reduce heat and simmer 1½ hours. Stir mixture frequently to prevent sticking. Immediately ladle into 2 hot pint jars, filling to within ¼-inch from the top. Adjust lids.

Process in boiling water bath 15 minutes. Start to count the processing time when water in canner returns to boiling.

Remove jars. Cool on wire racks 12 to 24 hours. Check jars for airtight seal (see Chapter 1). Makes 2 pints.

GREEN TOMATO CHILI SAUCE

1 lb. green tomatoes, peeled and cut up (4 or 5 medium)
1 lb. onions, peeled and cut up (4 to 5 medium)
1 lb. green apples, pared, cored and cut up (4 to 5 medium)
2 medium green peppers, seeded and cut up
1 tblsp. pickling salt
2 c. 5% acid strength white vinegar
2 c. sugar
2 tsp. dry mustard
1 tsp. ground mace
½ tsp. ground cinnamon
½ tsp. ground cloves
¼ to ½ tsp. cayenne pepper
6 to 8 drops green food coloring

Coarsely grind tomatoes, onions, apples and green peppers in food chopper. Place in large bowl; mix in salt. Let stand 4 to 6 hours.

Place vegetables in large kettle. Add vinegar, sugar, mustard, mace, cinnamon, cloves, cayenne pepper and food coloring; mix well. Bring to boiling. Reduce heat and simmer 1 hour 15 minutes or until mixture has the consistency of chili sauce. Stir occasionally. Immediately ladle into 3 hot pint jars, filling to within ¼-inch from the top. Adjust lids.

Process in boiling water bath 15 minutes. Start to count the processing time when water in canner returns to boiling.

Remove jars. Cool on wire racks 12 to 24 hours. Check jars for airtight seal (see Chapter 1). Makes 3 pints.

EASTERN CHILI SAUCE

2 medium tomatoes
1½ c. 5% acid strength vinegar
2 tsp. whole cloves
1 (3-inch) stick cinnamon
1 tsp. celery seeds
½ c. sugar
1 tblsp. chopped onion
½ tsp. cayenne pepper
½ c. sugar
1 tblsp. pickling salt

Wash, peel and quarter tomatoes.

Combine vinegar, cloves, cinnamon and celery seeds. Bring to boiling; remove from heat and let stand.

Combine half of tomatoes with ½ c. sugar, onion and pepper in large kettle. Boil 30 minutes, stirring frequently.

Add remaining tomatoes and ½ c. sugar to boiling tomato mixture. Boil vigorously 30 more minutes, stirring often. Strain vinegar; discard spices.

Add spiced vinegar and salt to tomato mixture and cook, stirring constantly, about 15 minutes or until of desired consistency. Pour into 2 hot, sterilized pint jars, filling to within ¼-inch from the top. Adjust lids.

Process in boiling water bath 5 minutes. Start to count the processing time when water in canner returns to boiling.

Remove jars. Cool on wire racks 12 to 24 hours. Check jars for airtight seal (see Chapter 1). Makes 2 pints.

SHORT-CUT CHILI SAUCE

3 qts. chopped peeled tomatoes
3 c. chopped celery
2 c. chopped onion
1 c. chopped green pepper
¼ c. pickling salt
2 c. sugar
¼ c. brown sugar, firmly packed
1½ tsp. pepper
1 c. 5% acid strength white vinegar
1½ tsp. mixed pickling spices

Combine tomatoes, celery, onion, green pepper and salt in large bowl. Let stand overnight. Drain in colander, but do not press vegetables.

Combine vegetables, sugars, pepper and vinegar in large kettle. Tie pickling spices in cheesecloth bag; add to kettle. Bring to boiling; reduce heat and simmer 15 minutes. Remove spice bag. Immediately ladle into 5 hot, sterilized pint jars, filling to within ¼-inch from the top. Adjust lids.

Process in boiling water bath 10 minutes. Start to count processing time when water in canner returns to boiling.

Remove jars. Cool on wire racks 12 to 24 hours. Check jars for airtight seal (see Chapter 1). Makes 5 pints.

BARBECUE SAUCE

8 lbs. tomatoes, peeled and quartered
2 large onions, peeled and quartered
2 green peppers, seeded and cut in strips
2 c. chopped celery
2 large hot red peppers, seeded and cut in strips
3 c. 5% acid strength vinegar
3 c. sugar
2½ tblsp. pickling salt
1 tblsp. dry mustard
½ tsp. ground red pepper
½ tsp. ground cinnamon
¼ tsp. ground cloves
½ c. Worcestershire sauce
½ to 1 tsp. bottled hot pepper sauce

Put tomatoes, onion, green peppers, celery and hot peppers in blender container, filling jar ¾ full. Blend at high speed 4 seconds; pour into large kettle. Repeat until all vegetables are blended.

Add vinegar, sugar, salt, mustard, red pepper, cinnamon, cloves, Worcestershire sauce and pepper sauce. Bring to boiling. Reduce heat; simmer 1 hour 30 minutes or until volume is reduced to almost one-half. Stir frequently. Immediately ladle into 7 hot pint jars, filling to within ¼-inch from the top. Adjust lids.

Process in boiling water bath 15 minutes. Start to count the processing time when water in canner returns to boiling.

Remove jars. Cool on wire racks 12 to 24 hours. Check jars for airtight seal (see Chapter 1). Makes 7 pints.

TACO SAUCE

About 24 hot red peppers
2 qts. peeled, chopped tomatoes (4 lbs.)
1 c. chopped onion
2 cloves garlic, minced
2 c. 5% acid strength cider vinegar
2 c. 5% acid strength cider vinegar
½ c. sugar
4 tsp. pickling salt
2 tsp. seasoned salt
1 tsp. dried oregano
1 tsp. dried basil

Seed and chop enough hot red peppers to make 2 c. (Wear rubber gloves to prevent burning hands.) Combine with tomatoes, onion, garlic and 2 c. vinegar in large saucepan. Cook 15 to 20 minutes or until vegetables are soft. Press through a sieve.

Combine sieved vegetables, 2 c. vinegar, sugar, salt, seasoned salt, oregano and basil in large saucepan. Simmer 1 hour 15 minutes or until thick. Stir frequently toward end of cooking. Immediately ladle into 4 hot, sterilized half-pint jars. Adjust lids.

Process in boiling water bath 10 minutes. Start to count the processing time when water in canner returns to boiling.

Remove jars. Cool on wire racks 12 to 24 hours. Check jars for airtight seal (see Chapter 1). Makes 4 half-pints.

WESTERN GOURMET KETCHUP

18 lbs. tomatoes
3 tblsp. pickling salt
⅔ c. sugar
1 tblsp. paprika
¼ tsp. ground red pepper
1 tblsp. dry mustard
1 tblsp. whole peppercorns
1 tblsp. whole allspice
1 tblsp. mustard seeds
4 bay leaves
4 hot peppers
1 tblsp. basil leaves
2 c. 5% acid strength vinegar

Wash, scald and peel tomatoes. Remove core and cut up. Cook in large kettle until soft. Press through a sieve. (Makes 7 qts. puree.)

Combine tomato puree, salt, sugar, paprika, red pepper and mustard in large kettle. Tie peppercorns, allspice, mustard seeds, bay leaves, hot peppers and basil leaves in cheesecloth bag; add to kettle. Bring to boiling. Reduce heat and simmer 1 hour 30 minutes or until thick. Add vinegar the last 10 minutes of cooking. Remove spice bag. Immediately ladle into 4 hot, sterilized pint jars, filling to within ¼-inch from the top. Adjust lids.

Process in boiling water bath 10 minutes. Start to count the processing time when water in canner returns to boiling.

Remove jars. Cool on wire racks 12 to 24 hours. Check jars for airtight seal (see Chapter 1). Makes 4 pints.

BLENDER KETCHUP

48 medium tomatoes (about 8 lbs.)
2 medium sweet red peppers
2 medium green peppers
4 onions, peeled and quartered
3 c. 5% acid strength vinegar
3 c. sugar
3 tblsp. pickling salt
3 tsp. dry mustard
½ tsp. ground red pepper
½ tsp. whole allspice
1½ tsp. whole cloves
1 (3-inch) stick cinnamon

Quarter tomatoes; remove stem ends. Seed peppers and cut in strips.

Put tomatoes, peppers and onion in blender container, filling jar ¾ full. Blend at high speed 4 seconds; pour into large kettle. Repeat until all vegetables are blended.

Add vinegar, sugar, salt, dry mustard and red pepper. Tie allspice, cloves and cinnamon in cheesecloth bag; add to kettle. Simmer in 325° oven or in electric saucepan until volume is reduced to one half. Remove spice bag. Ladle into 5 hot, sterilized pint jars, filling to within ¼-inch from the top. Adjust lids.

Process in boiling water bath 10 minutes. Start to count the processing time when water in canner returns to boiling.

Remove jars. Cool on wire rack 12 to 24 hours. Check jars for airtight seal (see Chapter 1). Makes 5 pints.

HOMEMADE FRUIT KETCHUP

12 tart apples, cored and thinly sliced
2 medium onions, finely chopped
1 c. sugar
1 tsp. pepper
1 tsp. pickling salt
1 tsp. dry mustard
1 tsp. ground cloves
1 tsp. ground cinnamon
¼ tsp. ground allspice
1½ c. 5% acid strength vinegar
½ c. water

Place apples in large saucepan. Cover with water. Cook until tender. Put through sieve.

Combine apples, onion, sugar, pepper, salt, mustard, cloves, cinnamon, allspice, vinegar and water in kettle. Bring to boiling. Reduce heat and simmer 2 hours 30 minutes or until thick, stirring frequently. Immediately ladle into 5 hot, sterilized pint jars, filling to within ¼-inch from the top. Adjust lids.

Process in boiling water bath 10 minutes. Start to count the processing time when water in canner returns to boiling.

Remove jars. Cool on wire racks 12 to 24 hours. Check jars for airtight seal (see Chapter 1). Makes 5 pints.

PLUM KETCHUP

6 lbs. purple plums, halved and pitted
2 large cooking apples, cored
 and cut up
1¼ c. 5% acid strength cider vinegar
2 c. brown sugar, firmly packed
2½ tsp. pickling salt
½ tsp. ground mace
⅛ tsp. ground cloves
1 (3-inch) stick cinnamon

Combine plums, apples and vinegar in large kettle. Bring to boiling. Reduce heat and simmer, covered, 15 minutes or until fruit is soft. Press mixture through sieve or food mill to remove skins.

Combine sieved mixture, brown sugar, salt, mace, cloves and cinnamon in kettle. Bring to boiling. Reduce heat and simmer 1 hour or until mixture is reduced to one-half. Stir frequently. Discard cinnamon stick. Immediately ladle into 4 hot, sterilized pint jars, filling to within ¼-inch from the top. Adjust lids.

Process in boiling water bath 10 minutes. Start to count the processing time when water in canner returns to boiling.

Remove jars. Cool on wire racks 12 to 24 hours. Check jars for airtight seal (see Chapter 1). Makes 4 pints.

GRAPE KETCHUP

5 lbs. Concord grapes
½ c. water
5 c. sugar
2 c. 5% acid strength vinegar
1 tsp. salt
½ c. mixed pickling spices

Combine grapes and water in large saucepan; bring to boiling. Put grapes and cooking liquid through sieve or food mill, making 9 c. pulp.

Combine pulp, sugar, vinegar and salt in large saucepan. Tie pickling spices in cheesecloth bag; add to saucepan. Bring to boiling; reduce heat and simmer slowly until thick, stirring occasionally. Remove spice bag. Immediately ladle into 4 hot, sterilized pint jars, filling to within ¼-inch from the top. Adjust lids.

Process in boiling water bath 5 minutes. Start to count the processing time when water in canner returns to boiling.

Remove jars. Cool on wire racks 12 to 24 hours. Check jars for airtight seal (see Chapter 1). Makes 4 pints.

SPICY CRANBERRY KETCHUP

2 lbs. cranberries
½ c. 5% acid strength cider vinegar
1½ c. water
3½ c. brown sugar, firmly packed
2 tsp. paprika
2 tsp. ground cinnamon
1 tsp. ground allspice
1 tsp. ground cloves
¼ tsp. pickling salt

Combine cranberries, vinegar, water and brown sugar in large saucepan. Bring to boiling. Reduce heat; simmer 5 minutes or until cranberries are soft. Stir occasionally. Put through a food mill or coarse sieve. Return to large saucepan.

Add paprika, cinnamon, allspice, cloves and salt. Simmer, stirring frequently, 5 minutes to blend flavors. Immediately ladle into 7 hot, sterilized half-pint jars, filling to within ¼-inch from the top. Adjust lids.

Process in boiling water bath 10 minutes. Start to count the processing time when water in canner returns to boiling.

Remove jars. Cool on wire racks 12 to 24 hours. Check jars for airtight seal (see Chapter 1). Makes 7 half-pints.

CHAPTER VII

Easy Freezer and Refrigerator Specialties

Harvest can be the season when minutes really count. But chances are you can still squeeze time to put up one of these fast-fix pickles or relishes. They are time-savers because you do not have to process them at all! Your refrigerator or freezer takes over the job of preserving them and their fresh flavor provides a bonus in good eating.

You can make Easy Sweet Dills and Refrigerator Bread and Butter Pickles for instance, and store them in the refrigerator, but use them within a month. They aren't quite as good, of course, as processed pickles, but they do have their own special fresh taste.

The second type of quick pickles are relishes and sauces that you can make and freeze. They will keep for 3 months. The colorful Frozen Gazpacho Relish pinch hits for a mixed vegetable salad. Or, it's refreshing as a frosty soup on a hot summer day.

REFRIGERATOR PICKLED BEETS

2 c. whole cooked or canned small beets, drained
¾ c. 5% acid strength vinegar
¼ c. water
3 whole cloves
1 (1-inch) stick cinnamon
1 slice lemon
1 slice onion
6 tblsp. sugar
¼ tsp. salt

Combine beets, vinegar, water, cloves, cinnamon, lemon, onion, sugar and salt in saucepan. Bring to boiling and boil 1 minute. Cool. Cover and refrigerate. Makes 1 pint.

REFRIGERATOR BREAD AND BUTTER PICKLES

3 c. cucumbers, thinly sliced (3 c.)
1 large onion, thinly sliced
1 c. 5% acid strength vinegar
¾ c. water
¾ c. sugar
1½ tsp. salt
½ tsp. celery seeds
½ tsp. mustard seeds
¼ tsp. garlic salt
¼ tsp. onion salt
⅛ tsp. ground turmeric

Combine cucumbers and onion. Pack into 2 pint jars.

Combine vinegar, water, sugar, salt, celery seeds, mustard seeds, garlic salt, onion salt and turmeric in saucepan. Bring to boiling. Reduce heat and simmer 5 minutes.

Pour over cucumbers. Cool. Cover and refrigerate. Makes 2 pints.

SHORT-CUT DILL SLICES

1 lb. cucumbers, sliced ⅛-inch thick (1 qt.)
¾ lb. onions, sliced and separated into rings (2 c.)
4 tsp. salt
2 tblsp. water
½ c. sugar
⅔ c. 5% acid strength cider vinegar
1½ tsp. dried dill weed

Combine cucumbers, onions, salt and water in large bowl. Let stand 2 hours. Drain, but do not rinse. Return vegetables to bowl along with sugar, vinegar and dill. Let stand until sugar has dissolved and liquid covers vegetables, about 45 minutes.

Pack into 2 pint freezer containers, filling to within ½-inch from the top. Cover; label and freeze. Makes 2 pints.

PICKLED PINEAPPLE

1 (1 lb. 14 oz.) can pineapple chunks
1¼ c. sugar
¾ c. 5% acid strength vinegar
$1/16$ tsp. salt
12 whole cloves
1 stick cinnamon

Drain pineapple, reserving 1¼ c. juice. Combine juice, sugar, vinegar, salt, cloves and cinnamon in saucepan. Simmer 10 minutes. Add pineapple chunks. Bring to boiling. Cool. Cover and refrigerate several days before serving. Remove cinnamon stick and cloves before serving. Makes 6 to 8 servings.

BEET RELISH

1 qt. small beets
3 large onions, peeled
3 green peppers, seeded
¾ c. 5% acid strength vinegar
½ c. water
1 c. sugar
1 tsp. salt
1 tsp. mixed pickling spices
6 whole cloves

Wash beets. Cook 20 minutes. Drain and peel.

Coarsely grind cooked beets, onions and green peppers in food chopper; place in large saucepan.

Combine vinegar, water, sugar, salt, pickling spices and cloves in small saucepan. Simmer 10 minutes.

Strain vinegar and add to vegetable mixture. Bring to boiling and simmer until vegetables are tender. Spoon into 4 pint freezer containers. Cool. Cover and refrigerate. Makes 4 pints.

FREEZER CHILI SAUCE

2 qts. peeled, cored, chopped tomatoes (12-15)
1 c. chopped onion (1 large)
1 c. chopped green pepper (2 medium)
¼ c. chopped hot red pepper (1 small)
½ c. sugar
1 tblsp. salt
2 tsp. ground cinnamon
2 tsp. ground allspice
1 tsp. ground cloves
1¼ c. 5% acid strength cider vinegar

Combine tomatoes, onion, green pepper, red pepper, sugar, salt, cinnamon, allspice, cloves and vinegar in large kettle. Bring to boiling. Reduce heat and simmer 1 hour 20 minutes or until thick. Stir frequently as mixture thickens. Immediately ladle into 2 pint freezer containers, filling to within ½-inch from the top. Cool. Cover. Label and freeze. Makes 2 pints.

FROZEN GAZPACHO RELISH

4 large tomatoes, peeled, cored and chopped (2 c.)
1 medium cucumber, peeled and chopped (1 c.)
1 large green pepper, chopped (¾ c.)
¼ c. chopped onion
2 tblsp. chopped parsley
1 large clove garlic, minced
1 tsp. salt
⅛ tsp. pepper
¼ c. 5% acid strength vinegar

Combine tomatoes, cucumber, green pepper, onion, parsley, garlic, salt, pepper and vinegar; mix well. Pack into 2 pint freezer containers, filling to within ½-inch from the top. Cover. Label and freeze. Makes 2 pints.

To serve as a relish: Thaw and drain.

To serve as a soup: Combine 1 pt. thawed, undrained relish, 1 c. chilled tomato juice and 2 tblsp. olive oil. Makes 4 servings.

FREEZER GARDEN RELISH

1 small head cabbage
2 medium onions, peeled and quartered
4 large carrots, peeled and cut up
2 green peppers, seeded and cut up
2 sweet red peppers, seeded and cut up
¼ c. salt
2 c. 5% acid strength vinegar
2 c. sugar
1 tblsp. mustard seeds
1 tblsp. celery seeds

Put cabbage, onions, carrots, green and red peppers through food grinder, using medium blade. Combine vegetables and salt in large bowl. Let stand 3 hours. Drain and rinse. Press vegetables in colander to squeeze out excess moisture.

Heat vinegar, sugar, mustard seeds and celery seeds in saucepan just until sugar is dissolved. Cool. Combine with vegetables. Turn into 4 pint freezer containers, filling to within ½-inch from the top. Cover; label and freeze. Makes 4 pints.

EASY SWEET DILLS

2 qts. dill pickles, sliced (8 to 10)
4 c. sugar
1 c. brown sugar, firmly packed
2⅓ c. 5% acid strength cider vinegar
4 tsp. whole allspice
1 tblsp. peppercorns
2 cloves garlic, crushed

Drain pickles and discard brine. Combine sugar, brown sugar, vinegar, allspice, peppercorns and garlic in large saucepan; bring to boiling. Simmer 5 minutes.

Add pickles; heat to boiling. Drain syrup from pickles; set aside. Return pickles to jars. Pour syrup over to cover. Cool. Cover and refrigerate. Makes 2 quarts.

FROZEN CORN RELISH

20 ears fresh sweet corn
1½ c. sugar
2 tblsp. mustard seeds
1 tblsp. salt
½ tsp. ground turmeric
1½ c. 5% acid strength white vinegar
2 c. water
1 c. chopped green pepper
1 c. chopped sweet red pepper
1 c. chopped celery
1 c. chopped onion

Place ears of corn in boiling water in large kettle. Boil 5 minutes. Cut corn from cob. Measure; there should be 10 c. corn.

Combine sugar, mustard seeds, salt, turmeric, vinegar and water in large kettle. Bring to boiling. Add green pepper, red pepper, celery and onion. Return to boiling. Simmer 4 minutes. Remove from heat and add corn. Cool. Pack into 6 pint freezer containers, filling to within ½-inch from the top. Cover; label and freeze. Makes 6 pints.

Index

Acetic acid, 9
Acid
  balance, 9
  -food ratio, 9
  level, 6, 10

Air bubbles, 13
  removal of, 13
Altitude Chart, 15
Apple(s)
  Chutney, Tomato/, 99
  Chowchow, 94
  Wedges, Curried, 63
Apricot(s)
  Pickles
    California, 64
    Peach and, 72

Barbecue Sauce, 106
Beet(s)
  and Horseradish Relish, 88
  Pickled, 51
  Refrigerator Pickled, 115
  Relish, 119
Best-ever Bread-and-Butters, 29
Best-ever Piccalilli, 92
Blender Ketchup, 109
Blueberries, Spiced, 65
Boiling water canner, 5, 6
  how to use, 11
  processing times using, 14
Botulism, 10
Brine-cured pickles, 6, 38-44
  brine strength, 6
  fermentation temperature
    range, 7
  Fermented Dill Pickles, 39
  floating vegetables, 7
  Four-day Sweet Pickles, 38
  to pickle, 42
  how to prepare, 6
  prevention of shriveled pickles, 6
  prevention of slippery pickles, 6
  scum removal, 7
  Sour Pickles, 44
  Sweet Pickles, 43
Brussels Sprouts, Pickled, 58

Cabbage Pickles, 61
California Apricot Pickles, 64
Canning Procedure(s)
  air bubbles, removal of, 13
  airtight seal, checking for, 15
  closing jars, 13
  cooling jars, 15
  filling jars, 13
  head space in jars, 13
  preparing jars and lids, 12
  salt, 9
  sterilizing jars and lids, 12
  washing jars and lids, 12
Cantaloupe Pickle, 66
Carrot(s)
  Relish, Country, 80
  Sticks, Spiced, 50
Cauliflower Pickles, Tangy, 55
Celery Relish, Peppy, 82
Cheerful Sweet Pickles, 26
Cherries, Pickled, 68
Chili Sauce
  Eastern, 104
  Freezer, 120
  Green Tomato, 103
  Hot, 102
  Short-cut, 105
Chowchow, 93
  Apple, 94
  Fish Fry, 95
Chutney(s)
  Mint, 98
  Peach, 97
  Tomato/Apple, 99
Clostridium botulinum, 10
Cooling jars, 15
Corn Relish(es)
  Frozen, 124
  Sweet, 84
  /Tomato, 85
Country Carrot Relish, 80
Cranberry(ies)
  Ketchup, Spicy, 113
  /Orange Relish, 96
  Spiced, 68
Crisp-as-ice Cucumber Slices, 23

Cucumber(s)
  enzymes in, 9
  pickling, 8
  how to prepare, 8
  how to select, 8
  slicing, 8
  waxed, 8
Curried Apple Wedges, 63
Curried Vegetable Pickles, 60
Curry Pickles, 30

Darkening of fruits, 9
  prevention of, 9
Darkening of pickles, 17
Dill Pickles
  Chips, Hamburger, 28
  Easy Kosher, 22
  Easy Sweet, 123
  Extra Good Sweet, 35
  Fermented, 39
  Fresh-pack, 20
  Slices, Short-cut, 117
  Sweet, 27
Dilly Green Tomato Slices, 47

Eastern Chili Sauce, 104
Easy Kosher Dill Pickles, 22
Easy Pickle Chunks, 33
Easy Sweet Dills, 123
Eggplant Relish, 83
Extra Good Sweet Dills, 35
Equipment, Canning, 11-12
  canner, 11
  containers for brining, 12
  jars, 11
  lids, 11
  small utensils, 11

Fermented Pickles, *see* Brined
  Pickles
  Dill Pickles, 39
Fish Fry Chowchow, 95
Four-day Sweet Pickles, 38
Freezer Specialties
  Chili Sauce, 120
  Corn Relish, 124
  Garden Relish, 122
  Gazpacho Relish, Frozen, 121
  Short-cut Dill Slices, 117
French Sour Pickles, 32

Fresh-pack Pickles, 7
  Dills, 20
Frozen Corn Relish, 124
Frozen Gazpacho Relish, 121
Fruit(s)
  how to handle fresh, 7
  how to prevent darkening, 9
  removal of decay, 8
  how to select, 7
  how to wash, 8
Fruit-Fresh, 9
Fruit Pickles, 62-78
  See also individual kinds
Fruit Relishes
  Apple Chowchow, 94
  Chutney, Mint, 98
  Cranberry Orange, 96
  Pickled Pineapple, 118
Garden Walk Pickles, 48
Golden Glow Relish, 86
Grape Ketchup, 112
Green Beans, Pickled, 53
Green Grapes, Spiced, 69
Green Pepper(s)
  Melange, Green Tomato
    100
  Slices, Italian Sweet, 59
Green Tomato(es)
  Best-ever Piccalilli, 92
  Chili Sauce, 103
  Pepper Melange, 100
  Slices, Dilly, 47

Hamburger Dill Chips, 28
Hard water, 10
  how to remove minerals from, 10
Head space, 13
Heat sterilization, 14
Homemade Fruit Ketchup, 110
Hot Chili Sauce, 102
Hot Dog Relish, 91

Ingredients used in pickling, 7-10
  fruits, 7
  salt, 9
  soft water, 10
  spices, 10
  sugar, 10
  vegetables, 7
  vinegar, 9

Iodized salt, 9
Italian Sweet Pepper Slices, 59

Jars, canning, 11, 12
   airtight seal, 11
   closing of, 13
   filling of, 13
   preparing, 12
   spoilage checks of, 16
   sterilizing of, 12
   storage of, 15
   washing of, 12

Ketchup
   Blender, 109
   Cranberry, Spicy, 113
   Grape, 112
   Homemade Fruit, 110
   Plum, 111
   Western Gourmet, 108

Lids, canning, 11, 12

Mint Chutney, 98
Mixed Vegetable Pickles, *See also* Vegetable Relishes
   Curried, 60
   Garden Walk Pickles, 48
   Relish, 87
Modern pickle recipes, 6
Mushroom Pickles, Party, 56
Mustard Sandwich Pickles, 36

Non-iodized salt, 9

Onion Hamburger Relish, 90
Onions, Pickled, 52
Open-kettle Canning, 6

Parsley Pickle Chunks, 34
Party Mushroom Pickles, 56
Peach Chutney, 97
Peach(es)
   Halves, Pickled, 71
   Pickles, 70
   Pickles, Apricot and, 72
Pear(s)
   Pickles, 73
   Rosy Spiced, 74
Peppy Celery Relish, 82
pH level, 6, 10

Pickled
   Beets, 51
   Beets, Refrigerator, 115
   Brussels Sprouts, 58
   Cherries, 67
   Green Beans, 53
   Onions, 52
   Peach Halves, 71
   Pineapple, 118
   Red Cabbage, 46
   Red Plums, 77
Pickles, *See also* individual kinds
   how to make successful, 5
   and Onions, 31
Pickling problems, 16-17
   dark color, 17
   hollow, 17
   shriveling, 16
   softening, 16
Pickling salt, 9
Pineapple Pickles, 75
Plum(s)
   Ketchup, 111
   Pickled Red, 77
Prize Sweet Pickles, 25
Processing times
   fermented or fresh-pack dills, 14
   other pickles, 14
Prunes, Spiced, 76

Quick-process pickles, 20-37
   See Fresh-pack pickles

Refrigerator Specialties
   Beet Relish, 119
   Beets, Pickled, 115
   Bread-and-Butter Pickles, 116
   Easy Sweet Dills, 123
   Pickled Pineapple, 118
Relishes, *See* Fruit Relishes, Vegetable Relishes
Ripe Cucumber Relish, 89
Rosy Spiced Pears, 74

Salt,
   canning, 9
   iodized, 9
   non-iodized, 9
   pickling, 9
Sauce(s) 101-113, *See also* Barbecue, Chili, Taco, Ketchup
Short-cut Dill Slices, 117
Sliced Cucumber Pickles
   Best-ever Bread-and-Butters, 29
   Crisp-as-ice Cucumber, 23

Curry, 30
Hamburger Dill Chips, 28
Mustard Sandwich, 36
Sweet Pickle Slices, 24
Sliced Zucchini Pickles, 57
Spiced Blueberries, 65
Soft water, 10
Spiced
   Carrot Sticks, 50
   Cranberries, 68
   Green Grapes, 69
   Prunes, 76
   Pumpkin, 49
   Sour Pickle Sticks, 21
   Vinegar, 43
Spicy Cranberry Ketchup, 113
Spoilage
   checks for, 16
   signs of, 16
Squash, Duo, Summer, 54
Storage of pickles, 15
Sugar used in pickling, 10
Summer Squash Duo, 54
Sweet
   Corn Relish, 84
   Dills, 27
   Pickle Slices, 24

Taco Sauce, 107
Tangy Cauliflower Pickles, 55
Tomato(es)
   Apple Chutney, 99
   Relish, Corn, 85
Vegetable(s)
   removal of decay, 8
   how to select, 7
   how to wash, 8
Vegetable Pickles, 45-61
   See individual kinds
Vegetable Relishes, 79-100
   Beet, 119
   Beet and Horseradish, 88
   Carrot, Country, 80
   Celery, Peppy, 82
   Chowchow, 93
   Corn, Sweet, 84
   Corn Tomato, 85
   Corn Relish, Frozen, 124
   Cucumber, Ripe, 89
   Eggplant, 83
   Fish Fry Chowchow, 95
   Freezer Garden, 122
   Frozen Gazpacho, 121
   Golden Glow, 86
   Green Tomato Pepper
      Melange, 100
   Hot Dog, 91

Mixed, 87
Onion Hamburger, 90
Piccalilli, Best-ever, 92
Zucchini Hash, 81
Vinegar, 9
   Homemade, 9
Watermelon Pickles, 78
Western Gourmet Ketchup, 108
Whole Sour Pickles, French, 32
Whole Sweet Pickles,
   Four-day, 38
   Pickles and Onions, 31
   Prize Sweet Pickles, 25

Yellow Cucumber Pickles
   Cheerful Sweet Pickles, 26
   Ripe Cucumber Relish, 89
   Sticks, 37

Zucchini Hash, 81
   Pickles, Sliced, 57